EARLY PRAISE

"Suzanne Eder possesses a rare combination of spiritual insight and logical pragmatism. *What You Want Wants You* will delight readers who enjoy exploring the mysteries of the world in practical ways. Suzanne allows us to test her beliefs in real-world settings, while offering her own inspiring perspective on each person's spiritual journey."

—Martha Beck, author of *The Way of Integrity*

"The depth of Suzanne Eder's wisdom is astounding and inviting, and you can access it here in this brilliant yet easy to understand book. Discover the real power you were always meant to experience."

—Thomas M. Sterner, author of *The Practicing Mind*

"This is the book and spiritual guidance we've been waiting for! Suzanne Eder unpacks how to manifest our deepest desires and she does it with laser-sharp intelligence, reverberating spiritual insight, and practical applications. Anyone who has been around the spiritual block will eat this up like pancakes! I could feel this book changing me as I read it. I could feel love elevating my brainwaves. *What You Want Wants You* is an absolute breakthrough."

—Tama Kieves, author of *Inspired & Unstoppable*

"In Suzanne Eder's new book, you will discover how to cultivate a manifesting consciousness as you reflect and open yourself up to unlimited possibilities, empowering you to pave the way to create the life you deserve and love. *What You Want Wants You* is a must read."

—Anita Moorjani, author of *Sensitive Is the New Strong*

"With the publication of her extraordinary new book, *What You Want Wants You*, Suzanne Eder immediately joins the ranks of the most important spiritual teachers writing today. Both supremely intelligent and immensely practical, this is a guidebook to the life you're meant to live, one you will read again and will recommend to everyone you know."

—Russell Martin, author of *Out of Silence*

"Suzanne Eder has written the thinking person's guide to the Law of Attraction. Here is theory and practice for honoring desire as the two-way street between the One Source and ourselves. Packed with helpful nitty-gritty for "the out-picturing of our thoughts," her new book demonstrates how to cut through the haze of "desire imposters" to perfect the question: what do I really, truly, want? She describes how to access your Expanded Self for an answer, and no years of esoteric training necessary! That Self is always with us if we open to it. *What You Want Wants You* is not just a sharing of useful methods to manifest on target, but a love song to the One Source who yearns—ardently, creatively—to see us receive what we want, so that it may better know itself through us. What a win-win for our lives!"

—Sue Westwind, author of *The Land Erotic*

WHAT YOU WANT
WANTS YOU

WHAT YOU WANT
WANTS YOU

*Saying Yes to Desire
as a Path of Awakening*

SUZANNE EDER

SAY YES QUICKLY BOOKS

Say Yes Quickly Books
7715 East Highland Avenue
Scottsdale, Arizona 85251 USA
https://sayyesquicklybooks.com

Ordering Information:
Special discounts are available on quantity purchases by corporations, associations, and others. For complete details, contact the "Special Sales Department" at the address above.

Cover background image: Adobe Stock
Interior typeface: EB Garamond
Author photograph by Thomas M. Sterner

What You Want Wants You / Suzanne Eder – First Edition
ISBN: 979-8-9872292-0-0

To my beloved parents, who are, no doubt, sending me love, light, and roses from beyond the veil. I love you always and forever.

Let yourself be drawn by the stronger pull of that which you truly love.

RUMI

The longing itself is its own fulfillment.

CONTENTS

INTRODUCTION

Welcome. I am honored and delighted that you're here. This book has been a work-in-progress for quite some time, and I offer it now with an open heart and the sincerest intention for it to illuminate, support, and uplift you. Most of all, I want you to come away with deepened trust in the inherent power, beauty, and integrity of your genuine desires.

The book comprises three parts. In part one, I present key concepts to support the understanding that saying yes to desire is a path of awakening to the fullness of who we are. These concepts are foundational to the material offered in the remainder of the book. Because of their conceptual and sometimes esoteric nature, I encourage you to read them at a relaxed pace, with a clear and open mind. If the concepts are unfamiliar to you, don't get bogged down by trying hard to figure them out. Invite your intuition to interpret their meaning and trust that you're integrating what is most relevant and helpful to you.

The chapters in part two provide an in-depth understanding of the nature of desire and how it manifests in our physical experience. I have placed particular emphasis on appreciating the role that emotions play in helping us shift our experience of manifesting what we want from one of struggle to one of ease. I have also made a point of highlighting common areas of confusion that many people have about how to leverage the power of the

Law of Attraction. My intention in part two is to help you feel clarity and conviction about how innately empowered you are to create a life you love, regardless of what others are doing.

In part three, I share several practices and exercises that have been very helpful to my students and clients in applying the principles of manifestation offered in the previous parts. They are designed to support you in cultivating a consciousness of genuine Self-Love, which is the quality of consciousness required for your heartfelt desires to manifest. I encourage you to allow your intuition to help you identify those that will be most helpful to you. Approach them with lightness of heart and steadiness of intention.

I have included a Reflection Point at the end of every chapter in the book. Each one is a concise presentation of the central message of the chapter. Give yourself quality time to reflect on the Reflection Points with a willingness to understand their meaning and implications.

Reflection is a key practice to support the embrace and embodiment of intellectual concepts you understand to be important. It is often overlooked or misunderstood in our busy, day-to-day lives. Without reflection, you may not be able to reach the deep levels of knowing that can significantly improve the quality of your lived experience. The choice to spend time in reflection is a wise, loving, and transformative one.

And now, we begin.

PART ONE

Foundational Concepts

1

BOW TO YOUR
SELFISH DESIRES

Desire is the impulse of Love to express itself.

At the age of thirty, shortly after my unexpected divorce—and my equally unexpected realization that I might have chosen a career that didn't suit me at all—I attended my first holistic expo. I was there at the irresistible urging of a dear friend who had secretly ventured into the murky and dubious territory known as "New Age." Its keynote speaker was an author whose understanding of life was far different than what I'd been taught—and far more appealing.

When she walked on stage I was transfixed. Never had I experienced in someone such a palpable, peaceful ...presence. At that time, it was an experience without a label. All I knew was that she radiated calmness, kindness, and wisdom, and I could *feel* it. I stood completely still, marveling at how tangible the feeling was.

And then, suddenly, I experienced an unexpected shift into an otherworldly dimension of expanded clarity. For one timeless moment, as I gazed at her and literally felt the energy of her presence, I knew with absolute certainty that I, too, was an author and a teacher. A clear and present desire was birthed within me to become what, in that paradoxical moment, I knew I already was.

As I shifted back into normal consciousness, the clarity of knowing I'd so powerfully experienced was muted. I understood only that something significant had happened. What I didn't yet know was that the fervent longing to write and teach had come back through the dimensional shift with me.

I was working as a certified public accountant at the time, and my analytical brain dismissed my newfound desire immediately; it was ridiculously improbable and completely out of line with the life I had planned for myself. Yet as hard as I tried to ignore or suppress it, it would not be ignored or suppressed. It kept nudging me to make different choices and explore different perspectives about life.

Those nudges eventually led to my transformation from corporate climber to fitness instructor to energy healer to transformational teacher, author, and personal mentor. Along the way, I have developed a completely different understanding of who we are and why we're here than I had at the start of the journey, one that keeps deepening and expanding. Yet at its core is something I found early in my journey of self-discovery—a sparkling revelation that ignited within me a resonant knowing and unfamiliar passion that changed the trajectory of my search.

Know thyself

This is the jewel I discovered:

The One desires to know itself in, through, and as the many, giving rise to this Universe and everything in it.

This life-altering perspective that we are each individualized expressions of the same source, which I now refer to as One Source and I recognize as Love, dovetails beautifully with a complementary perspective that resonates strongly with me. Each of us has a Divine spark within that animates our very being, and the path of enlightenment is a journey of waking up to that glorious truth.

One perspective reveals the passion of the One Source to express itself through the many. The other reveals the passion of the many to know and live the truth of their Oneness—their divinity.

Together, they tell us that our uniqueness as individuals is a direct consequence of the Divine desiring to express itself through all of us, and that the embrace of our personal desires not only leads to our greatest personal fulfillment, it fulfills the desires of the One Source from which we come.

*Imagine...*One Source wants passionately to experience its countless brilliant aspects through and as each of us, and that wanting—that desire—is the very impulse of creation. It is the impulse of Love to express itself, and the movement of Love into form is Life.

In other words, we exist *because* of desire.

As individual extensions of One Source, what we genuinely want is what One Source wants to create and experience through each of us. Can you feel the enormity of that? *What you genuinely want is what One Source wants.* It is what Love wants.

Your pure desires pulsate with Life itself. They are always seeking expression, which is what generates the impulse to create. Desire is sacred and vital to Life itself, and it has a life of its own that wants to express itself through you.

What you want, wants you.

The generosity of being selfish

As you consider desire from this perspective, it becomes apparent that the nature of desire is expansive and life-giving. Desire is the force that moves the Love of One Source into action, into Life. It is inherently and eternally generous, and it is the means through which One Source experiences its myriad qualities such as joy, harmony, beauty, abundance, balance, strength, grace, elegance, focus, organization, simplicity, artistry, precision, complexity, delight, and countless others.

Our individual desires to create things and experiences are the specific and diverse avenues through which One Source experiences those general attributes, which means that honoring our individual desires contributes to the ongoing expansion of the universe. *Your personal desires, and mine, are literally multiplying One Source's expression and experience of itself. We are expanding the Universe.*

Can you sense the profound significance of that? Your personal desires *matter*.

Yet many of us have been taught that personal desires are selfish, or at least subservient to the needs of the Whole. Our underlying unity is often interpreted to mean that we are more alike than we are different and that we all fundamentally want—or should want—the same things.

I see things very differently.

I understand that, as expressions of One Source, at our core we all want to experience the glorious qualities of that One Source. Who doesn't want to experience vibrant health, harmony, creativity, beauty, abundance, or any number of those countless One Source qualities? Yet my unique notion of beauty may be vastly different than yours, or I may be drawn to a life of simplicity while you are called to explore the richness of complexity.

And that's the whole point: we are not all supposed to want the same thing. We are here to bring our unique expressions of One Source qualities to life. It is through our infinitely diverse individuality that One Source continues to expand. *This is the magnificent yet mystifying paradox of our existence. We are One in essence yet many in expression.*

Exploring the paradox

There is growing awareness across all fields of learning of our connected-ness with each other and with our planet. In companion with that grow-ing awareness is a common belief that our connectedness is more im-portant than our individuality and that to preserve it, we must in some way sacrifice or otherwise tone down our individuality, which often trans-lates into toning down our individual desires. Many are forecasting immi-nent destruction if we don't all agree on how to move forward in service of the whole.

It is powerfully and poignantly true that we *are* all connected with each other and with our planet, and that our ongoing growth and evolution are tied to an ever-deepening understanding of this truth. Yet in recognizing our commonality, it's easy to lose sight of the value and purpose of our individuality.

This is because we often confuse our *interconnectedness* with our *underly-ing unity*, assuming them to be two expressions that mean the same thing when in fact, they do not. This misunderstanding can lead us to false con-clusions about the nature of desire and our relationship with it.

Let's go back to the paradox of our existence: we are one in essence, yet many in expression. One Source desires to know and express itself through and as the many. The *medium* of this expression—the creative medium of One Source, which is the vehicle of our interconnectedness—is energy. We are, as is everything in the Universe, vibrational in nature.

The properties of energy are such that, fundamentally, we are neither solid nor separate. We are patterns and fields of energy, translated by our senses into what we perceive as distinct physical beings with distinct physical parts. And unknown to many people, the nonphysical, experiential aspects of who we are—our thoughts, feelings, memories, beliefs, assumptions, perspectives, etc. —are also energetic in nature.

23

These nonphysical aspects of our experience are what I refer to as our personal consciousness. The energy of our personal consciousness is very real, although not generally perceivable through our physical senses. Utilizing more subtle sensory perception, clairvoyants, shamans, and mystics throughout the centuries have seen or sensed this energy, which may have been referred to as soul or spirit or aura.

Because of the various properties of energy—or vibration—our individual energy fields are not separate, although they are distinct. Their frequencies interact with each other to form an aggregate energy field. This is what is known as mass or collective consciousness, and because of it we are connected not only through our economic, ecological, social, and cultural systems, we are connected at a more profound and formative level through our consciousness.

Paradoxically, we are also individuals, each of whom has free will. We are distinct centers of awareness and perception, with the creative *ability* of One Source to direct the creative *medium* of One Source, which is energy, in ways that reflect our uniqueness. We effectively have control over our own personal energy fields, allowing One Source to experience itself in countless diverse ways through our free will choices.

Singular essence versus a collective of multiple expressions

Many people believe that the interconnectedness of our individual energy fields, which combine to form a single collective energy field, defines our unity. Yet there is a vast difference between the *underlying unity* or oneness of One Source, from which all of life comes, and the *surface aggregation* of our individual human energy fields, or consciousness, into a collective consciousness.

To help illustrate this vital difference, imagine that each of us is a differently colored and uniquely pulsating light. The radiance of our individual lights is powered by the same perfectly functioning energy source, of which there is an infinite supply.

Imagine further that each of us gets to choose the *degree* to which that powerful energy flows through us. The smaller the degree, the dimmer our light becomes. When all lights are fully open to the flow of this energy source, the resulting kaleidoscope of light is a marvel of beauty, complexity, and artistry. To the degree that some lights do not fully allow this source energy to flow, the kaleidoscope appears to be distorted, unbalanced or broken.

Although this image is a highly simplified one, I offer it to distinguish between the *unity or oneness of the underlying energy source* and the *aggregate of individual lights tapping into that source, which form a single visual tapestry.* The underlying energy source in this example represents the One Source of which each of us is an individual expression, and the observable kaleidoscope of light represents the collective consciousness of humanity.

What is vital to understand here is that our unity—our common source— is a given, a constant, an unchanging reality. There is nothing we must do or even *can* do to preserve this unity, because it can never be broken. It simply *is*, and the energy and substance of that One Source is available to us all. The essence of this One Source is Love, the ultimate reality, and from it the pure desire for self-expression emerges.

While we need not, and cannot, do anything to preserve the Oneness of Source, the incredible opportunity we have as individuals is to tap into it: to recognize its power and creatively use that power for our own self-expression, each in our own way and at our own pace. This is the essence of free will—the freedom of choice.

Our freedom of choice is so complete that we can choose thoughts and actions which may, or may not, be in harmony with One Source. Referring back to the lighted kaleidoscope metaphor, we can choose not to allow the source energy to flow, or to do so sometimes but not all the time. And so, the collective consciousness of humanity, which is an aggregate of our interconnected personal energy fields, reflects the vagaries of our individual perspectives. It is ever-changing, in contrast with the changeless essence of our One Source.

The only way the aggregate of human consciousness can change is through changes made by each of us individually, because free will exists at the level of the individual. This means that we can only make choices for ourselves. We cannot make them for others. Yet in making the most significant personal choice of all—the choice to align with One Source—we can lovingly influence others to do the same.

To the extent that any of us are individually in harmony with One Source—to the extent we allow that source energy to flow through us—our personal consciousness contributes to the upliftment of everyone through our shared group consciousness.

I think of this dynamic as feeding energy into the grid. As I cultivate states of being such as peacefulness, joy, harmony, and clarity, I reinforce those qualities in the entire grid of human consciousness. Their increased vibrational strength makes it easier for others to sense and experience those same qualities uniquely through themselves, much as a tuning fork calls forth its corollary vibrational tone from a nearby guitar string.

The point here is that *our maximum power as individuals flows through our personal connection with the One Source supplying all power*.

Yet because it's easy to confuse the *aggregate* of human consciousness with the underlying *oneness* of One Source, we often think that, to honor our unity, we should try to tune to each other rather than to One Source. And that often translates into trying to get everyone to agree with each other, which is fundamentally an unworkable strategy.

Agreement versus harmony

It might seem ridiculous to imply that trying to agree with each other is not a good thing, so let me be clear: I'm not saying we should actively promote disagreement. I'm saying that the only way to create a harmonious collective is through more of us making the personal choice to come into harmony with One Source. As more of us tune in more of the time, we generate an ever-stronger vibration of collective harmony because *One Source is always in harmony with itself.*

That's the key. Our unity is a given and a constant; we don't have to force or manipulate it into being by trying to get others to agree with us, or by compromising our desires to agree with them. One Source is always in harmony with itself, so *when we are in harmony with One Source, we have access to a vastly loving Intelligence that guides us toward and through harmonious interactions with others.*

When we try to negotiate or even force agreement with others, we often lose our own connection with One Source because many of the people we're trying to reach agreement with are, themselves, out of harmony with One Source. It happens all the time, in ways large and small.

It happens when your partner comes home from work in a bad mood, and you forego the warm bath you wanted because she petulantly demands that you watch a depressing crime show on TV with her—it's the least you can do after the day she's had—and you end up in a bad mood yourself.

It happens when you make a self-deprecating remark, so your friend will not feel envious of something wonderful you just experienced, and the comment reinforces doubts you have about your talent or abilities.

It happens when people in a group are outraged at an injustice and others in the group, who think they should be loyal to the group rather than to their own inner authority, join with the angry ones and say or do harmful things in revenge.

In these and countless other ways we try to force, manage, or manipulate ourselves into agreement with others, we feel out of integrity with ourselves. That's our signal that the approach isn't a healthy one. Trying to agree with everyone is neither possible nor helpful. Intending to be in harmony with One Source is the only sane path toward harmony with others, because only One Source can inspire us with the ideas, impulses and synchronistic opportunities that promote the kind of harmony we seek.

Now let's bring this back to desire and an understanding of why personal desires aren't selfish in the way that word is commonly understood. Intending to be in harmony with One Source is the path to our greatest harmony with others. Being in harmony with One Source necessarily and essentially includes the honoring of our personal desires to create, share or experience what we genuinely want, because our genuine desires are the desires of One Source to express itself.

We have now arrived at a whole new understanding of what it means to be Selfish:

Your personal desires are an expression of your true Self as an extension of One Source. They are vital to the expansion of the Universe and only you can honor them. As you do, your personal energy field or consciousness contributes to the field of human consciousness in ways that encourage others to be in harmony with One Source. *As more and more of us come into harmony with One Source, we naturally come into harmony with each other.*

This isn't pie-in-the-sky, it's practical

I had a vivid experience years ago that brought this truth home to me in a very direct way. I was on the leadership team of an organization that offered spiritual retreats on a regular basis, and the retreats were a significant component of its services. I had already hosted one very successful retreat and the founder of the organization, my boss, wanted me to host another one. A bigger one.

The only problem was, I didn't want to host another retreat. It simply was not a genuine desire of mine. Yet I waffled internally with the usual seesaw of "yes, but" thoughts that commonly arise when we have been conditioned to ignore our genuine desires in favor of conforming with others' expectations of us.

Finally, I gave myself permission to want what I really wanted, which was to say *no* to leading the retreat, and, ultimately, to walk away from that organization and reclaim my own business. I took the time to center myself in my truth before initiating our scheduled call to talk about the retreat. I reminded myself that my genuine desires were important and that, by definition, they served the Whole.

I made the call. And within seconds of our initial exchange of pleasantries, I felt myself shift into that dimension of expanded clarity I'd experienced before. I was still seated in my kitchen while talking on the phone, yet I was also somehow beyond that point in space and time. I could see the invisible hand of One Source, moving things around behind the scenes with great deftness, grace, and joyful purpose. Every element was vibrant and sparkling as new places and positions were assumed.

As I witnessed that incredible display of complex yet effortless orchestration, I heard my boss telling me that someone else had volunteered to lead the retreat, in a geographical location she had previously targeted for the ongoing expansion of her business. She was clearly excited about the new opportunity and the volunteer was delighted that my boss had said yes to her offer.

Needless to say, so was I. It was a simple yet clear reminder that our genuine personal desires arise from our oneness and are inherently in harmony with each other.

I realize it doesn't always appear that way, which is one of the reasons I'm writing this book. I want to help dismantle the distorted view of desire created by our false beliefs about who we are. But if you can set aside your objections for now, see if you can intuitively sense the validity of this premise of harmony within the One Source. Open to the possibility that as One Source expresses its immense love, wisdom, and power through each of us, an elegantly designed system is revealed:

What you genuinely want to express, experience, and create is what the world most benefits in receiving from you or experiencing with you.

What you personally desire may or may not be something that others see as beneficial to humanity, such as replanting trees in the rainforest. Yet the deeper truth here is that it doesn't matter how others view your desires. It matters that they feel genuine to you, because your genuine desires reflect the infinite intelligence and harmony of One Source. You are always doing your part when you are honoring what you want in your heart of hearts.

The ongoing process of nurturing true desires and bringing them to life is, in a very real sense, what life is all about. You could even think of it as your purpose for being here.

Why desire gets a bad rap

I believe desire often gets a bad rap, especially in spiritual circles, because many people—in falsely believing they are separate from One Source and feeling an inner void as a result of that belief—think they can fill the void with material things. As they come to realize that the pursuit of material gain is often a hollow one, that realization can lead them to conclude that personal desires are immature or misguided.

But what's easy to overlook is that the purpose of things we desire from a place of feeling separate from One Source is different than the purpose of things we desire from a place of alignment with One Source, even if those things appear to be the same on the surface. The problem isn't with desire itself, it's with the false belief in separation from One Source.

Desire itself is never the problem; forgetting who we are is the problem.

For example, consider a loving and confident woman who has joyful appreciation for color, pattern, texture, and style. She buys and wears clothes as an expression of her joy and artistry. Another woman, insecure and wanting desperately to fit in with others, buys clothes so that she'll be accepted by those who dress similarly.

Both women are buying clothes but are having vastly different experiences—and feeding vastly different energies into the grid of human consciousness. The purity and life-giving nature of desire is fulfilled through the confident woman's embrace of her unique gifts, and those qualities or frequencies are now strengthened in our collective consciousness. The insecure woman, doubtful of her worth and buying things to gain acceptance, is reinforcing thoughts of "less than" in the collective.

Into the rabbit hole—forgetting who we are

In the forgetting of who we are as extensions of One Source, we falsely believe ourselves to be separate from the infinite love, intelligence, and power of One Source, and separate from each other. The belief in our separateness gives rise to a belief in scarcity, because we perceive only individual things and people, of which there appear to be a finite number.

The belief in separateness also leads to assumptions that we can be "less than" something or someone else, and that we are inherently vulnerable to forces outside of us. It fosters in many of us a deep sense of unworthiness and a whole constellation of related false beliefs about our talent, value, and potential. In others it stimulates a perceived need to somehow prove their worthiness in order to earn their fair share of scarce resources, and the effort of trying to prove their worth—which is a given and therefore cannot be proven—is exhausting.

The false belief that we need to prove ourselves worthy of our fair share of scarce resources gives rise to a worldview of having to compete for them, which provokes a win/lose mentality. And where there is the possibility of loss, there is fear. There is also the need to judge winners and losers, good and bad, right and wrong. Fear and judgment walk hand-in-hand in a world where we've forgotten our divine heritage.

Fear and judgment, in their myriad forms, are the crushers of life-giving desire. And yet it's so easy to fall into condemnation of others, even for those of us on a spiritual path. For example, many people condemn what they view as overspending on material things. They attempt to shame or scare others into pulling back on what they want, arguing that there aren't enough material resources on our planet to accommodate everyone's desires (many of which have been judged as greedy).

In their condemnation of others, they forget that fear and condemnation can only exist in moments of forgetting who we really are, and that forgetting who we are is the cause of the problems we see.

They forget that what we focus on is what expands in our reality, and that focusing on what isn't wanted creates more of it.

They forget that the very foundation of this universe is unending Love, and that individual free will is freely given. It is meant to be explored and understood, not punished.

They forget that the vibration of condemnation is not harmonious with the vibrations of growth, generosity, and effective solutions. Condemning anything limits the creative expansion of All That Is.

Judgment can never dissolve judgment. Fear can never dissolve fear. Condemnation can never dissolve what is condemned.

In this example and countless others, the effective solutions we seek can only come to us through our connection with the infinite intelligence, power, and love of One Source. They cannot be accessed from a vibration of condemnation.

The *fact* of our unity isn't meant to corral us all into wanting the same things or to limit what we want. That is in direct opposition to the fundamental desire of One Source to express and experience itself through and as the many.

Yet through the *understanding* and *embrace* of our unity with One Source, we become empowered to create the diversity of things and experiences we want—and to do so in harmonious ways, because One Source is always in harmony with itself.

As we commit more deeply to the full remembrance of who we are, the inherently powerful and life-giving nature of our pure personal desires for peace, abundance and fulfillment lead us into the creation of a whole new world—just as our distorted personal desires, arising from fear and judgment, have created a world we wish to change.

Where do we go from here?

In chapter six we will take a closer look at how to recognize desire imposters that arise from the false belief in our separateness, and we'll explore a deeper understanding of the nature of our pure desires and how we can invite them into our awareness.

For now, take a moment to read and reflect on our first Reflection Point. Give yourself the gift of further reflection when you can set aside more time to do so. Open yourself to it through meditation, contemplation, or journaling. Ask yourself, "If this is true, what else might be true? What might this mean for me now?"

Reflection Point
I am a gloriously unique expression of One Source. My desires are the desires of One Source to experience itself through me, as me.

2

THE PRIMACY OF
CONSCIOUSNESS

*In a vibrational universe, the quality of your thoughts governs
the quality of your lived experience.*

I don't remember where I was first introduced to the idea that you
create your own reality, but I remember thinking it was both intriguing and obvious. It seemed obvious because I understood that we
each have the freedom to make choices that directly affect the reality of
our life experiences. Yet the fuller context of what I read at the time made
it clear the author wasn't talking only about the choices we make and the
actions we take. She or he was talking about our thoughts and beliefs as
the determinants of what we experience.

That was the intriguing part. It seemed radical, empowering, and terrify-
ing all at the same time.

The idea wouldn't leave me alone, and I began exploring it in earnest.
There were, and are, countless books and courses about how our thoughts
create our reality, many of which you've probably read or taken. My own
understanding of this concept has evolved over the years and is now an
integration and distillation of teachings from the brilliant minds of more
people than I can name, from scientists to channelers to energy healers to
New Thought ministers to enthusiastic students such as me, who followed their fascination into this strange new world. It has become funda-

mental to my life and my work, and it plays a vital role in the journey of awakening to the glorious truth of who we are.

A fresh look at an age-old concept

Depending on the nature of your religious or spiritual upbringing, the term "Holy Trinity" may have a very particular meaning for you, one that may or may not resonate with you now. In many Christian traditions, the Holy Trinity is understood as three distinct yet inseparable aspects of God: Father, Son, and Holy Spirit. The obvious exclusion of mother and daughter from this trinity led me initially to dismiss it once I reached adulthood. Yet as I continued along my own spiritual path, which is personal and not tied to any established religion, I uncovered references to trinity that started making sense to me.

What I now think of as the Trinity of Creation is my refreshed understanding of the Holy Trinity, the essence of which is an understanding that the creative power of One Source, often called God, has three distinct aspects. Yet because One Source is obviously and fundamentally One, those aspects are not and cannot be separated from each other.

The Trinity of Creation—or, more simply, the creative process—exists because of the powerful desire of One Source to experience itself *through* and *as* the many. The potent impulse for self-expression requires and therefore generates its own vehicle to move it from the nameless, faceless, boundaryless Beingness of Love—which you may have been introduced to as the Void, the womb of all creation, or the Field—into a state of existence in multiple forms. This can be thought of as movement from the inner to the outer, or in the words of physicist David Bohm, from the implicate to the explicate. The vehicle of movement is *intention*.

Intention is purpose and direction. It is a definite *yes* to the desire. It might also be thought of as the converter of energy potential into energy expressed, which, again, indicates movement. I understand it as the bridge between the unmanifest and the manifest, providing structure and purpose for the movement of desire into expression, much as the bed and banks of a river provide a structure within which water can flow in a particular direction.

Intention is the activator of this potent creative process. Through the power of intention, our desires have movement, direction, and purpose. As desire emerges from the field of infinite possibility into the outer world of existence, it becomes an idea, a mental construct. An idea is, in effect, its identity, its particularity, its uniqueness with respect to other desires emerging from the Void. Inherent within it is the intelligence required for its manifestation in accordance with its intention. It is a point of focus.

Idea is the first of the three inseparable aspects of the creative process.

Creation, being the manifestation of ideas into forms and experiences, requires a creative medium. The medium of creation in this universe is vibration or energy. Consider a potter sitting down at her wheel, intending to form a bowl out of the clay. "Bowl" is the idea that reflects a desire and intention for the creation of a specific thing, and the clay is the medium with which she works to create it. In the broader perspective of all creation, energy is the medium of creation. It is the "stuff" of which all perceivable things, both animate and inanimate, are made.

Energy is the second of the three inseparable aspects of the creative process.

Energy is directed into form through focus. It is the finished bowl in our physical analogy, and it is any number of "things"—distinct expressions of One Source—as perceived by individual perceivers. It is the expression or experience of the idea.

Manifestation is the third of the three inseparable aspects of the creative process.

All expressions of One Source, from the smallest subatomic particle to the largest structures in the cosmos, reflect and express the three inseparable aspects of the Trinity of Creation. You and I are the expression of the *idea* of "human" that originates in the divine mind of One Source. Through the creative medium of *energy*, our bodies, which are marvels of advanced harmonics, are formed in accordance with the intelligent design inherent in the idea. They are perceived and therefore experienced as the *manifestation* of a human body. We are idea, energy, and manifestation all at the same time, as is everything and everyone in the universe.

Everything is energy

Unlike the clay in the analogy of a potter at her wheel, the universal creative medium of energy forms literally everything—including the potter herself and her wheel. It is now widely understood scientifically that 99.99 percent of atoms are space. And that space within atoms and therefore within us—like the space between objects in our everyday reality, and the vast expanses of space visible in our cosmos— is not empty. It is filled with omnipresent electromagnetic fields.

This means that literally everything, including each one of us, is a configuration of multiple frequencies of energy. We are energetic, vibrational beings living in an energetic, vibrational universe.

This energy carries the intelligence and information required for all manifested forms to function in accordance with their purpose. In fact, we can think of energy as synonymous with intelligence and information, which I refer to as consciousness.

Consider a cell. Its frequencies of energy convey intelligence and impulses that relate to its function *as* a cell. This is what is known as cellular consciousness, or the energy field within which a cell has its being.

You can see that the intelligence and information required for the functioning of a human is distinctly different from that required for the functioning of a cell or a plant or a lizard or any other manifested form. Each manifested form has its own energy field—its own level of consciousness—and all energy fields are connected through a universal energy field.

Let's look more closely at the energy field, or consciousness, of a human. In addition to the energy fields related to the functioning of all the cells, organs, joints, tissues, systems, and processes that a human body requires, human consciousness includes additional information and intelligence related to our functioning as a whole person—our talents, skills, thoughts, beliefs, memories, assumptions, and conclusions, and the emotions associated with them. All these elements of our experience are energetic in nature because energy is the creative medium of One Source, and the totality of them within each of us is what I refer to as our personal fields of consciousness, personal consciousness, or personal energy fields.

Spiritual masters, mystics, energy healers, shamans, and clairvoyants across the centuries have seen and interacted with these nonphysical energy fields that science is only now beginning to acknowledge and measure. And they have learned some incredible things, one of which is that human energy fields can be intentionally shifted through *focus*. More importantly, they can be intentionally shifted into a coherent state. But coherent with what?

Coherent with the all-knowing, all-powerful, and all-loving energy of One Source—your Divine Essence—pulsing within you. One Source pulses at the heart of every atom of existence.

This pure energy is nonphysical and exists eternally, within and beyond space and time, which means it intersects with every point in what we perceive as space and in every moment of what we perceive as time. Yet for us to *experience* this energy in our physical lives, we must bring our personal energy field into harmony with it.

It might be helpful to think of your energy field as a vibrational screen or filter that can allow One Source energy to flow from the nonphysical into your physical experience or can block it from doing so. This filter can be calibrated to any point along the allowing/blocking continuum.

You calibrate your energy field by shifting your consciousness—your ideas, beliefs, thoughts, assumptions, conclusions, and worldview—in ways that bring it into vibrational harmony with the perspective of One Source.

This means that your personal consciousness is the gateway to the potent desires and nuanced streams of One Source intelligence that are ready to be expressed through you, as you.

The vital roles of focus and perception

The manifestation of a particular idea requires both a focuser and a perceiver of it. Let's use sound as an example. Sound is a concept or idea that originates in One Source, which I also like to think of as Divine Mind or Infinite Intelligence. Specific energetic frequencies are focused into existence by One Source (or by individual expressions of One Source, such as musicians), and are perceived through each of us as sound.

Without a perceiver to translate the frequencies into a recognizable something, the *idea* of sound has not *manifested*. This is the answer to the age-old question of whether there is a sound if a tree falls in a forest, and no one is around to hear it. The answer, from this perspective, is no. But there are waves of energy that are stimulated by the action.

A potter sitting at her wheel is both the focuser and the perceiver. She feels the desire to create, says *yes*, and her desire becomes an idea or mental image she intends to act on, and she forms it out of clay through her focused attention, her talent, and her purposeful actions. She can hold in her hands an object she recognizes as a bowl. Yet if someone comes into her studio who has never seen a bowl before and has no concept of it, that person does not see a bowl. She or he sees only an interpretation of what the potter has done with the clay, one that matches an idea or experience that person has already had.

The importance of "idea"

Remember that the manifest world arises from the unmanifest Void or womb of creation. The pulse of desire emerges from the Void through intention and becomes a particular idea. Without a particular idea, there can be no manifestation. So, in terms of the manifestation process, of the three inseparable aspects of the creative process, *idea* is primary.

For example, consider the idea of "blue jay" and imagine that you love blue jays. Endowed as you are with the creative power of One Source, you are a focuser and perceiver with the free will to choose where you focus and how you perceive things. Those choices determine what you manifest in your experience.

Since you love blue jays, thoughts of appreciation for them are active in your personal field of consciousness because you have focused repeatedly on them. Each time you think of or see a blue jay, your focus on it strengthens those thoughts of appreciation in your energy field.

One day, after several hours of working inside at your computer, you decide to take a break and step outside. You inhale the fresh air with relish and relax into appreciation for the gorgeous day it has turned out to be, after a gray and stormy morning. You feel so blessed to be outside, enjoying the beauty of nature right in your own back yard. Out of the corner of your eye you see a bird flying in from the left toward a tree that stands only a few feet from where you are. It lands on a branch that is in your direct line of sight and sits still, regarding you with curiosity. It is a blue jay. You smile with delight and say hello to the bird. It tweets in response and then flies away.

You manifested the specific idea of "blue jay" into your experience through your focus. Not because you were focusing on blue jays in that moment, but because you have repeatedly thought of them with appreciation, and those appreciative thoughts have a strong, active vibration in your consciousness. Through the powerful Law of Attraction, which governs all energy and draws similar frequencies to one another, the blue jay, itself a marvel of combined energetic frequencies, was drawn to you. You were in a state of appreciation for the beautiful day, and therefore you attracted more to appreciate.

You perceived it as a delightful experience because the *nature* of your thoughts about blue jays is one of appreciation. Others who, for whatever reasons, have a strong dislike of blue jays, will also attract them into their experience because of the strength of their thoughts about them. But the *nature of their thought* is dislike, so they perceive the blue jay as a nuisance or unwelcome distraction.

I offer this simple example to illuminate an essential understanding about consciousness, one that relates to the earlier point about *idea* being primary in the creative process. Our focus on any idea is what strengthens its vibrational power in our personal consciousness.

The word "idea," as I'm using it here, means any mental construct in our personal consciousness. Mental constructs include thoughts, beliefs, assumptions, conclusions, images, and memories. I include image and memory as examples because a mental construct does not have to be expressed in words. Images and, often, memories are mental constructs without words. All mental constructs are *ideas*. They are points of identification and focus, each conveyed through the medium of energy on its unique frequency.

The more frequently we focus on any given idea, the stronger its vibrational frequency becomes in our personal consciousness, and the more likely it becomes that objects and experiences of similar frequencies will be attracted to us.

Are you focusing on what you want, or what you don't want?

Up to this point, I've focused primarily on ideas that reflect specific desires emerging from the Void as the "kickoff point" of the creative process, but there are countless ideas we hold that are unrelated to our desires, or even contrary to them. This is because we have the freedom to think whatever we want to think. We have a *choice* about what thoughts to focus on.

Every thought we have is a vibration that, if strong enough, has the energetic attraction power to draw similar vibrational objects and experiences into our lives. This is the means through which the medium of energy generates manifestations. It's why someone who strongly dislikes blue jays will draw them into their experience even though they are disliked.

Let's step back now and consider the personal energy field or consciousness. It is a vibrational composite of every mental construct, and the emotions associated with them, that a person is focused on in the moment or has previously accepted as true. If strong enough, any of these thoughts can be the "kickoff point" for manifestation because, *idea*—or thought—is primary in the creative process.

What this means is that our personal consciousness—the totality of all the ideas or thoughts we have accepted as true—is the foundation of all manifestations in our personal life experiences. *Consciousness is the primary cause of all physical effects*. Can you sense the enormity of that?

Consciousness governs what we manifest and how we perceive it. It governs what we manifest because the Law of Attraction can only bring us objects or experiences that resonate with the frequencies of our dominant thoughts. Remember, everything physical is energy vibrating at frequencies that we *perceive* as physical.

Consciousness also governs how we perceive manifestations because perception is an *interpretation* of energy, and interpretation is a function of the mind, or consciousness. So, nothing can exist outside of consciousness. What we experience is, in a real sense, the out-picturing of our thoughts.

This is what it means to create our own reality.

Handle with care

The understanding that everything we experience is an expression or reflection of our own consciousness is monumental. It is phenomenally empowering. But it can also be confusing, and it can generate a painfully false and unhelpful conclusion if not approached with intelligence, kindness, and respect.

Imagine, for example, that because of the experiences you had growing up, you have concluded that you are weak and vulnerable. Highly active in your consciousness are thoughts of being vulnerable to threats of all kinds.

You aren't specifically thinking those thoughts all day, every day—or even on most days—but they remain active because you've focused on them repeatedly over time.

You need a new car, and you choose one that has many advanced safety features. You're not fully aware that, although you're making a choice you believe will enhance your safety while driving, your *dominant* vibration is one of vulnerability and the need to protect yourself from possible threats. And so, even though the new car you're now driving has advanced safety features, you get into an accident caused by another driver's inattentiveness to traffic signals.

In this example, the understanding that "you create your own reality" may be confusing because you believed you were fostering greater safety by purchasing a car with advanced safety features. Without the more finely tuned awareness of the vibration of your thoughts that comes with practice, you didn't know you were vibrating more with *accidents* than with safety.

And now for the potentially painful part. As you begin to understand the correlation between consciousness and manifestation, you may get frustrated or angry with yourself. You might blame or even condemn yourself for attracting a car accident.

Concepts of fault, blame and condemnation are among the most damaging of all vibrations. They can arise only in the misperception of ourselves as separate from One Source and the assumption, therefore, that we are lacking in some way. They are *never* helpful or life-affirming.

Although we can and do attract unwanted experiences into our lives, it is not because there is something wrong with us. It is because we are still learning the dynamics of the manifestation process.

The incredible opportunity each of us has is to become more fully aware of our power to create safe driving experiences—and everything else we desire—through an understanding of our true nature as expressions of

One Source and the vibrational essence of our being. And, too, as we grow in awareness, we also grow in our ability to see the big picture of our eternal nature. From that vantage point we can understand the beneficial increase in desire that unwanted experiences stimulate and choose not to judge them as wrong.

In other words, as we grow in the understanding of our true nature and the nature of the universe, our ability to manifest our desires with greater ease improves dramatically. We enjoy more of what we want and experience less of what we don't want. At the same time, we learn to suspend judgment of what isn't wanted, understanding that our recognition of it increases our clarity and focus on what *is* wanted.

Most of us were not taught these things and therefore haven't learned to apply them. It takes practice, as does anything that is beneficial for us to learn. The more we learn and the more we practice, the better at this we get, and the better our lives become.

Intention and the nature of consciousness: separation or unity?

Let's circle back to the idea that intention is the bridge between the unmanifest and the manifest. I previously wrote that intention represents purpose and direction, which it most certainly does. I also said that intention is a *yes* to the desires emerging from the Void. That is also true, but not all the time. It can also be a *yes* to other things as well.

Because of the primacy of *idea* (more broadly, consciousness) in the manifestation process, we can manifest things unrelated to our genuine desires. This is because we can have thoughts vibrating in our consciousness that are unrelated, or even in contradiction, to our desires.

Whether we manifest what we want or what we *do not* want, intention is involved. It is the *yes* that provides purpose and direction. But the *yes* isn't always a yes to our desires. *Anything we have accepted as true is, fundamentally, a yes to that something.*

That something can be any thought ever held because every thought ever held by anyone still exists as a vibration in the collective consciousness of humanity. The number of ideas we can potentially say *yes* to is staggering.

Let's go one step further. The thoughts we have *access* to in the collective consciousness of humanity, and therefore the thoughts we potentially could say *yes* to, reflect our awareness of *who we are*. When I am aware of myself as an extension of One Source, my awareness effectively shines the light on thoughts in the collective consciousness that harmonize with that awareness. I can choose to say *yes* to any of them.

I can say *yes* to my desires and *yes* to the nuances of One Source Intelligence flowing through me. I can say *yes* to my worth, *yes* to my value, *yes* to supportive thoughts, *yes* to creativity, *yes* to abundance, *yes* to happiness, and *yes* to countless wonderful, inspiring, and fulfilling ideas that are in harmony with the truth of my innate power and brilliance as a unique expression of One Source.

When I mistakenly perceive myself as separate from One Source, I have access only to thoughts that reflect that misperception. So, I might say *yes* to unworthiness, *yes* to scarcity, *yes* to competition, *yes* to uncertainty, *yes* to doubt, *yes* to blame, *yes* to condemnation, and *yes* to all kinds of thoughts in the collective consciousness that aren't helpful, but which seem true from this vantage point of separation.

So, my *yes* in any given moment is either a *yes* to my talents and desires and supportive thoughts about them, or a *yes* to something other than that. Either way, my *yes* evokes purpose and direction. It becomes an intention. It activates vibration within my personal energy field and initiates movement.

There are a few key points of understanding here:

> It is always intention that activates the creative process.

Intention is a *yes* to a thought and it initiates vibrational movement in the direction of that thought.

Our awareness and understanding of *who we are* gives us access to the thoughts in the collective human consciousness that support and reflect that understanding.

This means that when we understand ourselves to be extensions of One Source, we have access to thoughts in the collective consciousness that support our desires. Our *yes* to those thoughts—our intention—activates those thoughts in our personal energy field, or consciousness. I call this "unity consciousness" because it vibrates in harmony with the understanding of our unity with One Source.

Unity consciousness yields the manifestation of our desires.

When we do not understand ourselves as extensions of One Source, we have access only to thoughts in the collective human consciousness that reflect that perceived separation. Our *yes* to those thoughts—our intention—activates those thoughts in our personal energy field, or consciousness. I call this "separation consciousness" because it vibrates in harmony with our perceived separation from Source.

Separation consciousness yields the manifestation of things and experiences we do not want.

I present unity and separation consciousness as two very broad, opposing categories to simplify the basic concept that intention—saying *yes* to thoughts of a particular nature in the collective human consciousness—is what determines the quality of our personal consciousness. And of course, the quality of our personal consciousness determines the quality of our personal manifested experience.

Please know that this isn't a one-and-done thing, or a one-time choice to say *yes* to something and then live with it forever. In our lived experience, all of this is very fluid and changeable. I can, in one moment of feeling deeply connected to One Source, say *yes* to something I know I want, and in that moment my personal energy field is vibrating in unity consciousness and attracting thoughts of positive expectation. Thirty minutes later, I can find myself saying *yes* to a doubting thought that I activated when I read something unsettling. In that moment, my personal energy field is vibrating in separation consciousness and attracting thoughts of negative expectation.

As I learn to strengthen and stabilize my focus on thoughts that are supportive of what I want, I gain vibrational momentum toward its manifestation. This is true for all of us.

Take a moment now to breathe deeply and invite your mind to be still. When you feel ready, reflect on the following:

Reflection Point

Consciousness is the primary cause of all physical effects. Physical objects and experiences exist only through consciousness and cannot be separated from it.

3

THE SIGNIFICANCE
OF THE ONE

*One Source is, and can only ever be, in harmony with itself
as it expresses through the many.*

I can still recall the vividness of a long-ago moment, experienced while I was reading Ernest Holmes' classic *The Science of Mind,* when a sudden and vast inner knowing expanded into my awareness. I felt currents of energy coursing through me and all around me, vibrating with a sense of this new inner knowing that, paradoxically, felt instantly familiar. In that timeless moment I somehow understood the unfathomably profound implications of there being only *One* Source of all creation.

Up to that point, my understanding of the oneness of Source had been just that—an understanding of a concept. In that moment, the concept revealed itself to me as a truth, one that challenged what I had previously accepted as true without fully realizing that I'd done so.

Consider deeply this spiritual truth that mystics and masters have spoken of for millennia: there is only One Source of all creation. There is no other creative power that can diminish or extinguish One Source, or even oppose it. Opposition cannot exist within the reality of One Source.

As we allow ourselves to reflect on the truth that there is One Source of All That Is, we realize something significant, obvious, and utterly profound, yet easy to miss: the concept of good versus evil is inherently flawed. We have been taught that evil is a force separate from good, with the ability to overpower and even eliminate good. We've been conditioned to believe that there is a source of good and a source of evil—two forces, not one, vying for supremacy.

The chaos and disruption that ensue from this conditioning is, perhaps, the intended message in the story of Adam and Eve being thrown out of the Garden of Eden. In versions of the Bible that describe the tree from which the infamous apple was taken as the tree of the *knowledge of good and evil*, I believe the word "concept" could be a more accurate translation than "knowledge." We cannot truly *know* of something that doesn't exist. But we can form a mental concept of it.

As individual expressions of One Source, we have the freedom to think in whatever ways we want to think, regardless of whether our thoughts are in alignment with the truth of One Source (unity consciousness) or not (separation consciousness). And because consciousness is the foundation of all manifestation, the powerful concept of good versus evil in our collective consciousness generates manifestations that reflect the concept. These manifestations are painful, sometimes horrifically so. Yet they are temporary, as are all physical manifestations. The unassailable oneness of One Source is the unchanging reality from which all experiences emerge and return.

One and one*ness*

As we further reflect on the existence of only One Source of All That Is, its "oneness" reveals another truth that is easy to overlook. And so, there are two significant implications that arise from the truth of One Source:

The first, as we've just explored, is that there is only One Source of All That Is, not two or more. This one creative power can never be extinguished because there is no other power to oppose it. Without opposition, its existence is eternal, and its creative power is infinite.

The second is that the One is, and can only ever be, in harmony with itself, even as it expresses through the many. Its oneness—its indivisibility—means that as it expresses itself through and as the many, the numerous individual expressions are extensions *of* the One; they are not and cannot be separate from it.

Our seemingly contradictory experiences to oneness

Our individuality—our existence as distinct beings with our own centers of awareness and perception—stimulates the expansion of All That Is. Through our diverse interactions with each other, fresh desires for new experiences arise naturally. These experiences, or manifestations, are differing frequencies of energy.

In our physical dimension of existence, these frequencies are perceived as what we call physical manifestations, or physicality. The physical dimension has the greatest degree of specificity of form of all levels of existence.

The specificity and stability of manifestations in the physical dimension is significant because with it comes the possibility of perceiving separation. Our physical senses cannot perceive the nonphysical energies of One Source that have extended themselves into the physical dimension. And if our understanding of who we are is limited to what we perceive through our physical senses, we believe ourselves to be separate from each other and from One Source.

Here is one of my favorite metaphors to illustrate this dynamic. Imagine you are a whitecap on the ocean, and all you can see of yourself is the whitecap, and that's all you can see of others, too. You can't see or feel the vast ocean of which you are an extension. You just see a lot of separate whitecaps bobbing along, some bigger than others who, at times, appear to consume the smaller ones. Whitecaps come and go; they're here and then they're not. You draw conclusions about your vulnerability as a single, small whitecap at the mercy of the bigger whitecap bullies or the nameless darkness all around you, not realizing that, fundamentally, you are the ocean. The *ocean*.

This metaphor has obvious limits to its relevance, as all metaphors do, but the understanding here is that while we are individuals, we are not separate from the One Source of our existence. Literally nothing we can perceive through our physical senses is separate from One Source. When we perceive ourselves as separate from One Source, we may conclude that we are vulnerable or unsafe or "not enough" in some way, as in the whitecap metaphor. This is how the concept of unworthiness arises.

Similarly, when we perceive things other than ourselves as separate from One Source and separate from each other—when we see specific things with edges and boundaries—by definition, we can also perceive their *absence*. This is how concepts of lack and scarcity arise.

The perception of separation from One Source—and its attendant conclusions of unworthiness, vulnerability, scarcity and lack—gives rise to all manifestations that are painful to experience.

Bringing it back to desire

Let's step back and consider all of this as it relates to desire. Desire is the very impulse of Love —the One Source—to express and experience itself through the many. I refer to each of the many individuated expressions of One Source here in the physical dimension as a Local Self. At the Local Self level of existence, our personal desires are the desires of One Source, now *expanding* its experience of itself through each of us.

Personal desires in our Local Self experience are stimulated in three ways:

Through the awareness of our innate talents and proclivities—our unique One Source qualities—that pulse with the desire for expression.

Through the natural diversity of life, which stimulates the identification of our personal preferences.

Through the pain or discomfort of perceiving and therefore experiencing some type of lack (the absence of something wanted), which stimulates desire for relief from that pain.

An example might be helpful here. Imagine that, in your current job, you discover you have a natural talent for encouraging and supporting others. You enjoy your work and take pleasure in helping others feel more confident and successful in theirs. This is your awareness of an innate desire to express a particular aspect of Divine Intelligence pulsing within you.

One day you stumble on an article about the explosive growth of the coaching industry and realize that you could potentially start your own business as a coach. The idea sparks your imagination, and you feel drawn to it. A fresh desire has been stimulated by your observation of the diversity of work experiences that utilize your talent, and the realization of a preference for self-employment.

Fast-forward a couple of years. You've started your own business and have continued to educate yourself on the ins and outs of being self-employed. Articles everywhere highlight the high failure rate of new businesses, many of which don't make it past the five-year mark. Focusing on those reports, you feel concerned about the growth rate of your business and begin thinking it may not gain the momentum it needs to carry you beyond that pivotal milestone.

You start noticing what isn't going well in your business and become concerned about your bank balance. It becomes increasingly difficult to cover your expenses each month. You now have a strong desire for financial abundance, stimulated by the experience of lack.

In later chapters, we'll take a closer look at how the manifestation of lack can occur and how we can more consistently shift our experiences toward what we want rather than the lack of it. What I want to emphasize here is that *desire is always calling us in the direction of One Source*, which is eternally expanding into more of All That Is.

Desire is what prompts us to joyfully express our innate intelligences and talents; it is what invites us to expand into new experiences that will satisfy us in new ways, and it is what calls us back to the harmony and abundance of One Source when we have mistakenly perceived ourselves as separate from it.

Is pain necessary?

The inaccurate perception of our separateness from One Source has been called, among many things, our fall from Grace, implying that we somehow made a mistake. We sinned. Many spiritual teachers, both ancient and modern, have endorsed this perspective. Others, thinking logically that if nothing is separate from One Source, which itself is Infinite Intelligence, then even our painful experiences are somehow part of the design. After all, how could Infinite Intelligence make a mistake? Some of these teachings go so far as to conclude that we reclaim our awareness of who we really are only through painful experiences.

Neither of these perspectives has ever felt quite right to me, even as I recognize aspects of validity in both. Over the years I've circled around and around this pivotal question of whether our perception of separation from One Source is a tragic mistake that we need to correct, or an integral part of a divine plan that ultimately supports our freedom and absolute well-being.

In other words, is pain necessary for growth?

In moments of deep inner stillness, I have come to understand that it is not a question of necessity but of possibility. The powerful desire of One Source to experience itself through the many, and the establishment of free will at the level of the individual, generates the *possibility* of perceiving separation and, in that perception, experiencing pain. But because there is only One Source, One Power—and it is Love—only good can ultimately come from any experience. Pain always gives rise to desire for relief from pain, and this intensified desire calls us powerfully back to One Source.

In other words, the painful perception of ourselves as separate from One Source contributes to the expansion of All That Is because it *amplifies* our life-giving desires to experience what our connection with One Source provides. In that way, it is beneficial, even if not necessary in the way the word is normally used.

Perhaps a fitting metaphor for Life is a grand, eternal experiment or adventure—a continual expansion of awareness that naturally leads to an infinite diversity of experience. There is no end point toward which All That Is reaches. There is only unlimited exploration, feedback, expansion and growth, the underlying intention for which is the expression of Love. *Life is the movement of Love into form.*

So, while we can and do grow in self-awareness through painful experiences, painful experiences aren't required for awakening to the truth of who we really are. We can, consciously and intentionally, choose to open more and more to the truth of our One Source nature, and live from that inspired, adventurous, and joyful place.

A continuous expansion of awareness

What makes this challenging is that painful thoughts of vulnerability, scarcity and lack continue to vibrate powerfully in the collective human consciousness, as they have for thousands of years. Generation after generation of humans has accepted them as true and passed them on to their children, not understanding the power of thought to create the reality we experience.

These painful beliefs and experiences cannot, however, affect our underlying unity with One Source. There is only One Source, one Power, and it is Love. While we can temporarily *experience* the pain of perceived separation, it can never become a permanent condition because the eternal reality is Oneness. And the power of pure desire that arises from painful experiences has the full force of Love in it. It is always in harmony with One Source and always moves us in the direction of One Source.

So, rather than seeing our perception of separateness from One Source either as a mistake or as a requirement for growth, I understand it now as a level of perception that gives rise to certain kinds of experiences. As our ability to perceive beyond the physical deepens—which is the same thing as saying as we wake up to more and more of who we are—we gain access to different kinds of experiences. These new experiences reflect the expanded possibilities that become available with our expanded self-awareness.

The quality and timing of this waking-up process is as unique from person to person as are our fingerprints because we each have free will, which lets us choose where, when, and how we focus our attention, and how we interpret what we perceive. Within any one of us, it's also unique to the various areas of our lives, depending on how we've come to perceive ourselves in each area. Most of us find it easier to come into harmony with One Source in certain areas than in others.

The point is that—even though we're now in the process of waking up to more and more of who we are as gloriously unique expressions of One Source—we still have moments or experiences that feel painful to us because, in those moments, we've lost that perspective. When we stumble into those painful experiences, how we interpret them determines whether we continue on a path of pain or move toward a path of ease. We can choose to see them not as evidence of our ineptness or of the unfairness of the world, but as catalysts to wake us up to the bigger truth of who we are.

They catalyze us by stimulating a desire for relief from the pain—a desire for peace or ease or abundance or support or joy or any number of qualities that move us away from what we're experiencing and toward what we want. Within that desire is the knowing that we are worthy of its realization. As we recognize and claim our worthiness, we learn to support our freshly honed desires rather than to diminish them.

We support our desires by bringing our thoughts into harmony with them. A deep understanding of the truth of our oneness with One Source is profoundly helpful in the process of finding harmonious thoughts.

The importance of reflection

The understanding that our patterns of thought create our lived experience through the powerful Law of Attraction is immensely empowering. It encourages us to pay more attention to the way we think and to cultivate patterns of thought that are in harmony with what we want.

Yet without a keenly felt understanding of the truth and reality of our oneness with One Source, it's easy to fall back into believing that what we've observed over millennia is real and true—a primary example of which is the belief that good and evil are separate forces that always and inevitably lead to conflict at all levels of our experience, from the personal to the global.

That belief and countless others, such as beliefs in our ineptness or powerlessness, are based on a false premise of more than one source of creative power. As I contemplate the truth that there is only *One* Source of all that is, not two or more, and that I am an extension of that powerful source, I find it easier to dismiss painful yet convincing beliefs that would argue otherwise.

This is the power of deep reflection. Because energy follows attention, when we reflect on this profound truth of our oneness with *the* creative power of the Universe, we strengthen our belief in it, and in ourselves as creators. In the absence of deep reflection, our attention continues to be absorbed in *what is*—what has been manifested to date—much of which reflects beliefs in the false premise of multiple sources of power. Choosing intentionally to reflect on that which affirms our worthiness and empowerment is a wise and loving choice.

Pause now and take a few deep breaths. When you feel ready, reflect on this Reflection Point:

Reflection Point

One Source is the only creative power in the Universe, the essence of which is unending Love. There is no other power in the Universe that can diminish or extinguish the power of One Source. I am an individual extension of One Source, imbued with its creative power.

4

THE ETERNAL NOW

Your creative power exists only, and ever, in the present moment.

You have no doubt heard about the power of now. It is important to the teachings of Eckhart Tolle, as well as those of Abraham, Seth, and many other spiritual and metaphysical teachers. For me, the understanding of it is both mind-blowing and comforting, an unusual but welcome combination.

As I studied and explored the power of now, I began capitalizing the word to distinguish it from the meaning of "now" that is most common. Rather than referring only to this immediate point in linear time— "I've got to do this right *now!*"—it signifies the eternal nature of our existence and the creative power available to us in every moment.

The eternal Now is the home of One Source. The present moment, defined not by the clock but by the quality and duration of our focus on any given thought, thing, or experience, is a portal between our limited experience of a moment in linear time and the timeless potentials that exist, eternally, in One Source. Our unmanifested desires are among these timeless potentials.

Manifesting in the now

Think of your pure desires as *possibilities*. They have yet to manifest, so, relative to where you are now, they are possibilities rather than realities. Your dominant thoughts about those possibilities determine the *probability* of your desires being realized by you, here in the physical dimension. The more resonant your thoughts are with the possibilities of your pure desires, the higher your probability is of manifesting them.

Now let's shift perspectives from where you stand in linear time, in which your desires are possibilities, to the eternal Now. From this view, your desires can be understood as very real. They are a real aspect of *you*.

Your desires are not separate from you; they are an expression *of* you, just as you are an expression of One Source. They exist on nonphysical frequencies, but they are real. Each one is vibrating with the full vitality of Life, as all desires do, which means each desire pulses with its full potential for physical realization. It is analogous to a seed holding the full potential of the plant.

You can think of the eternal Now as a distinct dimension in which your desires exist. Because of its eternal nature, it exists outside of what we experience as space and time. And because there is no separation within One Source, this dimension of desire is not separate from the physical dimension. This means that your desires, already existing in the reality of the eternal Now, intersect with your physical experience in every moment of time and in every point of space.

The opportunity you have in the physical dimension is to *experience* the realization of your desires through your physical senses, which you do moment to moment. Imagine a series of moments that can be connected, one to another, in a line. This line is what you experience as linear time. As mentioned above, I'm using the word "moment" not to convey a unit of measurable time but rather any amount of time in which you have a particular focus.

Each moment is a portal to your desires in the eternal Now, and your focus determines whether the portal is open or closed. Your focus in the moment further strengthens the vibration of whatever you're focused on. As the Law of Attraction responds to your focus, it draws resonant thoughts—either familiar ones from your personal field of consciousness, or similar ones from the field of mass consciousness—to the thoughts you're focusing on. In each moment, you are strengthening vibrations in your consciousness based on your focus.

Depending on which thought patterns you're focusing on, you are either increasing the probability of manifesting a desire or increasing the probability of manifesting something else. When any thought pattern has been strengthened sufficiently, it becomes strong enough to attract the vibrations you perceive in your experience as physical manifestations.

If a strong thought pattern is in vibrational harmony with a desire pulsing in the Now, it serves as a channel or conduit through which the desire flows powerfully from the eternal Now into your physical experience *right now*, as the blue jay did in the example I offered in chapter two.

If a strong thought pattern is not in vibrational harmony with any desire pulsing in the Now, the manifestation reflects the thought pattern itself which—because it is not in harmony with desire—is unrelated to anything you want.

What does this have to do with power?

Reflect now on the idea that every moment is a portal to your very real desires, pulsing in the Now. In the eternal Now, all your desires exist simultaneously. This means that *you can access desired outcomes, which are eternally vibrating in the Now, in any given moment.*

You don't need to have a long string of consecutive moments to create an outcome, because you have access to the entirety of your desires in the Now, in *any* moment. The string itself—the construct of linear time—has no inherent power of its own.

Note the distinction between where the power truly *is*—within the innately powerful, life-giving desires pulsing in the eternal Now—and the progression of moments in which you *experience the unfolding* of your desires. It is a subtle yet vital distinction. Desires don't manifest because you've given them a certain amount of time. Desires manifest because their inherent life-force energy impels them to manifest. And at the Local Self level you *experience* their manifestation in physical form when you learn to consistently bring your thoughts into harmony with them.

So, the amount of time involved is the time it takes for you to do that—to consistently bring your thoughts into harmony with your desires until those thoughts are dominant in your consciousness. This creates the conduit or open gateway through which your powerful desires flow from the eternal Now into the here-and-now physical experience of your Local Self.

Now let's consider a different kind of power that's involved in the manifestation process. There is a distinction between the innate, life-giving power of all pure desires, and the powerful Law of Attraction that strengthens whatever thoughts we focus on, whether they are in harmony with our desires or not, by adding resonant thoughts to them.

To experience our desires, we must focus consistently on thoughts that harmonize with them so that the powerful Law of Attraction can strengthen those thought patterns into conduits through which our desires can flow into our physical experience.

Through that same consistency of focus, we can and do manifest things unrelated to our desires because the Law of Attraction will bring us more of what is vibrating strongly in our consciousness, regardless of whether it is in harmony with our desires.

So, the power of the Law of Attraction is always active, whether we're manifesting what we want or what we don't want. Yet the innate, life-giving power of *desire itself* becomes available to us when our thoughts are in harmony with our desires, which gives a special boost to the manifestation process.

This "desire boost" is what creates the ease and flow we long to experience in our lives, and we'll explore it in greater depth in later chapters. For now, I want to clarify that our Local Self, present-moment power has two components:

The innate power of desire itself, which we don't control but that benefits us greatly when we're in harmony with it, and

The power of the Law of Attraction, which we also don't control but we can direct through our focus.

At the Local Self level, our job—our opportunity—is to mindfully and intentionally exercise our ability to focus, moment to moment. And, of course, we can exercise that ability only in *this* moment. So, in any moment, our Local Self focus activates thoughts that are in some degree of harmony with our desires, which are pulsing with the ultimate power of Life in our eternal Now.

To the extent we are in harmony with our desires in any given moment, we experience something pleasurable or satisfying or delightful or fulfilling in that moment (like the blue jay). And we strengthen the vibrational thought patterns that increase the probability of more of what we want flowing to us in future moments.

To the extent that we are *not* in harmony with our desires in any given moment, we experience something unwanted or confusing or frustrating (or any number of experiences other than delightful ones). And we strengthen the vibrational thought patterns that increase the probability of experiencing more of what we don't want in future moments.

Your point of power is always Now because:

Your ability to *focus* can only be exercised now.

The present moment is the only Local Self moment in which you can *experience* the unfolding realization of your powerful desires, pulsing eternally in the eternal Now.

There is no inherent power in the progression of linear time. It is the vehicle through which you experience the manifestation of your desires.

If time has no inherent power, can I manifest instantly?

In a very real sense, we're manifesting "instantly" all the time. Every experience we have is an in-the-moment manifestation of a dominant vibration in our consciousness, and our opportunity is to become more aware of, and intentional about, the thought patterns that are active in our consciousness. But we have the power to manifest what we want more readily and more easily than we typically believe we can, and it doesn't have to take a long time, once we understand the dynamic power of our desires pulsing in the eternal Now.

I'm not saying you could, with this understanding of the power of the Now moment, heal a chronic condition instantly or triple your income in a week—although I'm not saying you couldn't. Those kinds of outcomes *are* possible because you desire them; they exist in the eternal Now. But they are improbable, given your current thoughts about them. Since we experience our lives in linear time, the strengthening of thought vibrations to a manifestation point normally does take time.

What I want to emphasize is that the fact of your having experienced something unwanted for a long time has no direct bearing on how quickly you can change it. *The amount of time it takes has nothing to do with time itself and everything to do with the strength and stability of the vibration you're able to hold, moment to moment.* As you get better and better at focusing on what you want, your ability to turn possibilities into probabilities gets stronger and stronger.

You might have lived with an unwanted circumstance for a long time, but it needn't take an equally long time to turn it around because linear time has no inherent creative power. Bestselling author Anita Moorjani's stunning return to perfect health in a matter of hours, after years of battling cancer, is a powerful example of this.

Her situation was extraordinary, yet it highlights what is possible when your Local Self consciousness is in complete harmony with the truth of your oneness with One Source. You effectively open a clear channel through which your desires flow, unimpeded, from the eternal Now to the here-and-now of your physical experience, swiftly and easily. The power is in the desire itself. Your Local Self ability to focus opens the channel through which it can flow.

Typically, this kind of outcome requires persistence in shifting your focus, which doesn't always come quickly, so I don't want to paint a picture of instant manifestations as the norm. But I do want you to experience greater empowerment and ease in creating what you genuinely want in your life. When you have a deeper understanding of the inherent power of desired outcomes *already existing* in the eternal Now—and of your ability to access that power through your intentional focus—you experience more of what you want and less of what you don't want.

Don't I need to forgive my past before I can have a joyful future?

My exploration of the eternal Now stimulated insights into another aspect of creating lives we love that has been profoundly helpful, and that aspect is forgiveness. To be more specific, it's an understanding that forgiveness of the past, as many of us have been conditioned to understand it, is not a prerequisite for living a joyful life. Committing to the cultivation of a consciousness in harmony with One Source is, however, essential.

The essence of forgiveness is the release of judgment of someone or something, including ourselves. That release can only and ever occur in the present moment, and only when our consciousness is vibrating with love. Yet many or even most of us have not yet learned to *stabilize* our Local Self consciousness at that level, and so in any moment in which we're not vibrating there, we attract thoughts about our past that are, once again, resentful and blaming.

If we think of forgiveness as being directed to specific people or events that occurred at specific times, we then must forgive each person or instance all over again. Can you imagine how arduous the task would be of going back through your past to forgive anyone and everyone who ever hurt or disappointed you? And then to have to do it again in some future moment when you're feeling resentful again? Not to mention the fact that, in the moments of doing that exercise, you would have to focus on memories of the kinds of things you do not want, thereby keeping them active in your vibration.

It is only through the ongoing cultivation of a consciousness of harmony with One Source, moment to moment, that we free ourselves from thoughts of guilt, blame, and resentment, *regardless of whether those thoughts are about the past, the present or the future*. When we're vibrating with love, we see our past through the eyes of compassion, not judgment. And we see our future with trust in the goodness of Life.

A corollary to this is that we only feel guilt or blame or resentment-about our past when we feel those emotions in the present. When we're vibrating with those feelings, we feel badly about everything, not just our past. The vibration of those feelings colors everything we remember, everything we perceive and everything we expect.

So, we don't need to "go back" and forgive anyone and everyone who has ever hurt us before we can be free and happy. It's not even possible to do so. There is no going back, there is only Now.

And when we focus on events we have associated with pain in our past, we keep painful vibrations active in our powerful present moment. We're not accomplishing what we want to accomplish, which is a Local Self consciousness in harmony with our desires.

Cultivating that harmonious consciousness moment to moment, to the best of our ability and with lightness of heart, is the most loving commitment we can make to ourselves and everyone in our world. And that's what we'll continue to explore in this book.

I realize there are countless ways to nurture forgiveness that have helped many people over the years, and I am in no way denying the benefits they have provided. If you have a comforting and helpful understanding of forgiveness that is different from what I'm offering here, stay true to what works for you.

I offer this perspective because I've worked with many people over the years, myself included, who got tangled up in beliefs about forgiveness that were profoundly unhelpful and kept them stuck, with more self-judgment than ever. These fresh insights I have gained about forgiveness through my exploration of the eternal Now have been liberating for all of us. I offer them to you with that same heartfelt intention.

The gift of time

You might be surprised to learn that modern day physicists do not agree on what time *is*. We all experience ourselves moving through time, with a past, present, and future, but what, exactly are we moving through?

Years ago, I read one scientist's identification of time as a construct of the human mind, which fascinated me and felt somehow *true* in ways I didn't yet understand. As I've explored various ideas and experiences of time, I've come to think of it as a purposeful construct of the physical dimension, which originated as an idea in the Divine Mind of One Source. We experience this construct through the perceptual interpretations of our minds. Most importantly, the purpose of time, in our physical dimension, is a loving one:

The experience of linear time gives us the opportunity to savor, *and it gives us the opportunity to develop mastery of our* focus.

Here is a simple example. Let's say you love to host parties, and you have a desire to host a party with people who come from very diverse backgrounds. If this desire manifested as quickly as desires do in nonphysical dimensions, you would have the idea and then—voila! —the party would be underway.

You would have missed out on the satisfaction of playing with ideas for the party's venue and theme, deciding who to invite, creating the invitations, and letting new ideas to make it even more fun bubble up as it approaches. You would have missed out on the delightful synchronicities that brought ideas, resources, and people together in perfect timing as your desire unfolded, moment by moment.

In other words, you would have missed out on the creative process itself. The creative process is where most of the fun happens and where all the juicy momentum builds for the realized event.

Depending on how finely honed your initial idea was, you might also find yourself at your instant party with too many people in too small a space, many of whom really don't like parties and would rather be home, and with everyone else bickering over the paltry amount of food on the buffet table. In that moment, you might realize that time's role in slowing down the planning was very much your friend.

So, the construct of linear time is meant to serve our growth and satisfaction in the physical dimension. It effectively slows down the manifestation of our desires so we can *experience* the delightful coming together of the many aspects and elements of those desires. It also gives us an opportunity to actively participate—to feel and focus and choose—each step along the way.

A wonderful metaphor for this slowing down was offered by a fellow student in a class we were attending. He described how, as a child, he and his friends would go inner tubing in a fast-moving stream. They would deliberately put their legs in the water in such a way as to slow themselves down. In doing so, they could truly enjoy the ride—the sensations and the scenery and the motion itself—and enjoy it safely.

Like the fast-moving stream the boys floated in, the frequencies of energy that we perceive as physical are, in a real sense, fast-moving streams of energy/consciousness that our perceptive apparatus have effectively slowed down for us so we *can* perceive them. And our perception of them, moment by moment by moment, is the reality we experience—the journey. Destinations we reach along the way stimulate fresh desires for new experiences, and the journey continues.

Time is an inseparable aspect of the physical dimension; it is coexistent with it. It is meant to enhance the satisfaction, uniqueness, and specificity of our experience in this dimension. Time is a means through which we perceive and therefore experience fast-moving streams of consciousness, just as the children's legs were the means through which they slowed down their experience of the fast-moving stream.

Continuing with the stream metaphor, note that the water continues to flow even though the children don't move at its pace. A twig in the stream would move much faster than they would, not having any legs to slow itself down. So, there is a gap of time and space between the children and their destination.

Likewise, fast-moving streams of consciousness, which we perceive through a slowed-down lens of time, continue to flow. The flow of Life is always in motion, and we are effectively traveling at a different pace. So, in this physical dimension there will always be a time and space gap between where we are now (where we perceive ourselves to be) and where the streams are headed—which is always toward our desires.

This gap can be misinterpreted as evidence that we're somehow falling behind, when, in truth, we couldn't physically be anywhere other than where our physical senses perceive we are. In our misinterpretation of the gap between where we are in this moment and where we're going, we incorrectly construe time as a powerful entity that is separate from us, marching inexorably forward and either ignoring us or dragging us along against our will.

Thinking of time this way is hardly a recipe for an inspired, grace-filled, and fulfilling life. That's why I'm offering a broader perspective that emphasizes our creative power in every moment, and that places linear time in the role of enhancing our experience of desire fulfillment in the physical dimension.

"But what about aging and death?" you might ask. "Isn't it often true that we get sick or die before we've manifested our desires? Don't we literally run out of time?"

Yes. And no.

Yes, people often *do* get sick or die before they manifest their desires. And no, they don't run out of time. They shift their focus from the physical dimension back to the nonphysical dimension of One Source, in the eternal Now.

The topics of sickness and aging are immense, and a focused exploration of them in the context of vibration and the eternal Now would require its own book. But the principles and techniques of manifestation we're exploring can be applied to both because, like every other human experience, they reflect the dominant vibrations in our consciousness about them.

We can learn to cultivate a consciousness that supports vibrant health and ageless vitality, just as we can learn to cultivate a consciousness that supports financial abundance, creative self-expression, and whatever else our hearts desire. And we can start in any moment.

But we will never be done. Our desires, pulsing in the Now, are eternal. Unfulfilled desires from one lifetime can be realized in another, and new desires continue to arise because desire is the very impulse of Love— infinite and eternal—to experience itself. There is no destination, no end point. There is only creating and experiencing, creating and experiencing, creating and experiencing, in endlessly unique ways.

And yes, we will have a death experience relative to the physical body we're currently in. All of us will leave the planet with desires still pulsing in the eternal Now, yet to be fulfilled. That's why it's important to understand that life really is about the journey and not the destination, *because there is no destination*. It's why we serve ourselves extremely well when we live as fully as we can in each moment, because *this* moment is where Life is unfolding for us.

And it is why time is our friend in the physical dimension. Time gives us the opportunity to make one choice now, and a different choice later. It gives us the opportunity to practice focusing on what we want until we learn to do it masterfully, with trusting and joyful anticipation. It gives us the opportunity to savor the countless delightful details and synchronicities of our ever-evolving, ever-unfolding desires.

Time *is* the journey.

Spend some time reflecting on this chapter's Reflection Point, below:

Reflection Point

All creative power exists in the present moment. There is no creative power in the progression of linear time. Time is the vehicle through which we perceive the unfolding of our desires.

PART TWO

Principles of Manifestation

5

JUST SAY YES

No desire is too small to matter or too large to embrace.

I was a dozen years into my corporate career, climbing the proverbial ladder with steady determination. I was also the co-owner of a beautiful fitness studio where I taught classes two evenings a week and on Saturday mornings. The pivotal experience I described in chapter one, during which I suddenly realized a longing to be a teacher and writer, had happened several years earlier. Having convinced myself that I should focus on my serious career in accounting and let go of the frivolous notion that I could be a writer and teacher, I had purposely dismissed it.

What I didn't yet know was that it hadn't dismissed me.

I remember coming home one evening after work, tired and grumpy, and finding two magazines in my mailbox: the *Journal of Accountancy* and *Shape*, a magazine devoted to fitness. I held one in each hand and, as I looked at the *Journal of Accountancy*, I felt deflated. I knew I should read it but just couldn't bring myself to do it. A wave of guilt washed over me, but it wasn't strong enough to push me through my resistance. I sat down and devoured the *Shape* magazine instead.

A short time later, I was in my office perusing a catalog of continuing professional education courses, a certain number of which I had yet to complete to maintain my status as a certified public accountant. Again, I felt deflated and was acutely aware that I had absolutely no interest in any of the courses.

At that time in my life, I had tentatively acknowledged to myself that I enjoyed my role as a fitness instructor far more than I enjoyed my role as a corporate analyst. Yet I viewed my fitness instruction as a side job and remained committed to my "real" career.

Sitting in my office that day with the course catalog in my hands, a crack began to form in my commitment. Sneaking through that tiny crack was a strange, new thought: I could choose to let my status as a CPA lapse. After all, I wasn't serving the public as an accountant and my corporate career had migrated away from accounting and toward finance. I didn't need to be a CPA to do my job well, nor was it a requirement for the position.

That had been true for a while, but I had continued to take the continuing professional education courses to prove to company leadership, and to myself, that I was a professional committed to excellence. And having become increasingly unhappy with working at that company, I had also continued taking them to keep my options open for other jobs.

Yet in that moment, those reasons seemed contrived and unconvincing. The fresh idea had ushered in a sense of release that was so welcome and refreshing, I couldn't ignore it. I didn't know anything about the power of desire, but I knew, somehow, that choosing not to enroll in the courses was the right choice for me.

The nature of desire

Although I didn't understand it this way at the time, what I had done in that moment was to give myself permission to want what I knew, in my heart, I really wanted. I wanted to liberate myself from the CPE courses.

What I also didn't understand at the time was that the immediate desire to liberate myself from those courses was related to my bigger-picture desire to be a writer and a teacher. I had covered that one up, but its innate pulse toward realization kept emerging through whatever cracks in my thinking it could find. It was leading me, step by step, into my vision.

It is what all desires do. They keep finding ways to get our attention, so we keep having new opportunities to say *yes* to them. I said *yes* in that moment, then *no* again in many succeeding moments, but the desire itself never gave up on me. It kept looking for those cracks until, finally, I had enough momentum going in the direction of my desire that I actively jumped on board.

Pure desires are impulses to *experience* ourselves as the uniquely brilliant expressions of One Source we are. They are all about creating, expressing, and sharing, and they joyfully utilize our innate Divine talents and proclivities. In contrast, what I often refer to as desire imposters are things (or experiences) we pursue to prove something or to avoid something unwanted. We'll take a closer look at the imposters in the next chapter, but I offer the concept here to further illuminate the nature of what I'm calling pure desire.

In the story I shared at the start of this chapter, my pursuit of a successful corporate career was a desire imposter. I had convinced myself I wanted it, but my real motivation was to prove myself to others and to make enough money to avoid the unwanted experience of financial lack.

The desire to write and teach, which had revealed itself to me during that long-ago conference, was a pure desire to *experience myself as* a teacher and writer, to create teachings and books from my innate Divine talents and share them with others. That desire has fueled my evolution from fitness instructor to energy healer to transformational life coach to Alchemy of Self Love teacher and writer, and the evolution continues.

Pure desires are of the heart. They arise from and through Love, the foun-dation of Life. They are translated through the mind into specific ideas that manifest through the Trinity of Creation, as we discussed in chapter two. Identifying a desire as an idea is often the starting point of bringing our consciousness into harmony with it.

Pure desires light us up; they feel "right" or inspired or expansive or interesting or enlivening or perhaps all those things. They feel good. They reveal themselves to us through impulses, ideas that inspire us, and moments of recognition or deep knowing, such as the moment in which I recognized my longing to teach and write.

Pure desires come in all shapes and sizes, from simple preferences to lifelong passions. No desire is too small to matter or too large to embrace. They arise in all areas of our lives, not just in our jobs or careers.

One of my favorite stories of the realization of a pure desire is that of a friend of mine, whom I'll call Joy. I've come to think of Joy as an elegant manifester, because she seems naturally to know how to relax into the process and allow the perfect outcome to come to her.

At one point in her life, when Joy was renting a room in a friend's home, she longed to live in a place of her own. She had a clear vision of living in a charming cottage nestled in natural surroundings, even though those kinds of homes were typically priced well beyond her budget. Her intuition told her that her presence and talents would be welcomed and valued by the owner of the property.

I encouraged her to want what she really wanted, even though it didn't seem like a probable outcome when looking at the numbers. Joy, being the elegant manifester she is, stayed connected with her pure desire and the clarity of the intuition she'd received about it. And within a short amount of time, the seemingly improbable outcome become very real.

Joy learned that a woman with whom she worked was looking for a tenant for her carriage house, which was situated in a stunningly beautiful, bucolic setting. The woman and her husband were more concerned about finding someone they could trust than getting top dollar for their jewel of a carriage house. Joy was the answer to their prayers. They agreed on a rental price she could afford, and during the time she was there her landlords benefited greatly from her cooking and pet-sitting skills, as well as her overall caring and loving presence.

Joy trusted the life-giving potency of her pure desire, pulsing in the eternal Now to guide her to the perfect outcome. I think she had some doubts along the way, but they clearly weren't strong enough to get in the way of the desire's delightful realization. She didn't force herself to consider other housing options just because they were affordable. She stayed true to what she really wanted. And in doing so, she opened the channel through which her desire could flow effortlessly into her experience.

Joy's experience perfectly illustrates that honoring our desires opens us to greater ease, flow, and fulfillment. This is the "desire boost" I referred to in chapter four, and I've experienced or witnessed countless examples of it in my life and in the lives of my clients. It reveals itself as the fluidity of movement we experience when we allow the vast intelligence of One Source to orchestrate the coming together of things. It's not as much about speed as it is about ease and satisfaction, although things can and do flow into our experience more quickly when we're not pushing against them.

And the desire boost applies to all desires, not just the ones we think of as "big." Honoring desire is an *orientation* to life that yields greater ease and satisfaction in all areas and moments of our lives.

The desire boost

Imagine two streams. One is flowing toward its destination, which is your desires, and the other is flowing in the opposite direction. You are in the stream flowing away from your desires. You've found a way to turn your boat around and paddle furiously against the current toward what you want. It's exhausting and sometimes you stop paddling, but then your boat starts drifting with the stream, away from your desires, and you start paddling again.

Finally, you notice the nearby stream, flowing in the direction you want to go. After a few tries, you manage to get yourself out of the water. You drag your boat to the stream flowing toward your desires, push it in the water and jump in. With the paddles lying untouched on the bottom of the boat, you enjoy being carried by the flow of the stream toward your desires.

The ease of flowing toward your desires—compared to the struggle of pushing against an opposing current—is made possible by what I've been calling the desire boost. The boost comes from the desire itself, calling you joyfully toward it with the full force of Life. In this metaphor, the direction of the streams represents the direction of your thoughts. As you learn to bring your thoughts into harmony with your desires—which you can think of as pointing your thoughts in the direction of your desires—you flow with the powerful stream of Life toward them.

This metaphor can help us understand several things about desire and our relationship with it, starting with this: Just as it would be unnatural for two side-by-side streams to be flowing in opposite directions, it is unnatural for us to resist our own desires. It has become "normal" for us to do so because of our conditioning, but it isn't natural. Desire itself, moving from the infinite potential of One Source into multiple expressions as Life, creates a natural momentum toward realization. Only thoughts arising in separation consciousness can create momentum in the opposite direction.

The metaphor also reveals that we generally can't change streams—we can't change the direction of our thoughts—instantly. Some effort is required to get ourselves out of one stream and into the other. The effort required to change the direction of our thoughts is the cultivation of a consciousness of Love, which requires that we practice holding loving and supportive thoughts. We'll explore that in depth in the following chapters, but I want to emphasize here that the effort is worthwhile, and it doesn't have to feel like a struggle. Once we're in the stream we want to be in, life becomes more ease-filled and satisfying.

Finally, the stream metaphor illustrates another nuance of the relationship between thought and desire: when we're exhausted or frustrated as we paddle against the current leading away from our desire and we put the oars down, we drift further away. We may have let go of the immediate struggle, but we're still in the same stream of resistant thought. Getting into the stream of harmonious thought requires intentionality, focus, and practice.

We do have to put the oars down, of course. We must stop struggling so we can think clearly, shift focus and get in the other stream of thought. But letting go of the struggle without a clear and loving intention to get in the desire stream is tantamount to giving up on the desire. In truth, that isn't possible because our desires won't give up on us. Yet we can keep ourselves apart from their realization for a long time if we stay in the stream flowing away from them.

Here is an example of how that might be experienced. If I believe that "Life isn't fair," and that belief vibrates powerfully in my consciousness, I'm metaphorically paddling against that stream of thought in my life. Through willpower, I keep trying to get what I want but I never quite succeed, while others, who seem to have unfair advantages over me, succeed easily. At some point, I may conclude that I'll *never* get anything I want because life isn't fair. I may give up trying altogether, and, if so, the stream will carry me from resentment to cynicism and all the way to depression.

Of course, our point of power is always Now, and we can make the loving commitment to get in the desire stream in any moment, from wherever we are. Sometimes the worse we feel, the more compelled we feel to make that commitment, which benefits us enormously. Regardless of when we decide to get in the desire stream, it's helpful to know what to do after putting down the oars.

Acknowledge your desires

This is so fundamental it's easy to overlook, especially given how masterful many of us have become at talking ourselves out of what we really want.

We believe our desires are unattainable and so we try to content or distract ourselves with other things. But before we can get in the stream flowing toward our desires, we must acknowledge them.

Often, we don't know—or we think we don't know—what we want. If this sounds familiar to you, here are three suggestions to explore:

Ask yourself how you want to feel.

You may not know exactly *what* you want to create, experience, or share in your life, but you almost always know how you want to feel. For example, if you feel underutilized and underappreciated in your current job, you may not know what kind of work you'd love to do, but you know you want to feel fully engaged and appreciated. If you feel anxious or worried much of the time, you know you want to feel at peace. If you often feel impatient or frustrated, you know you want to feel relaxed and trusting.

Knowing how you want to feel, and having a clear intention to experience that feeling, might be all you would ever need to live an ease- and grace-filled life of deep satisfaction. I have a client, whom I'll call Jessica, who initially came to me with a singular desire to be at peace. She had struggled with worry almost all her life and knew there was a better way to feel and to live.

With her clear intention in place to live a peaceful life, we identified and shifted the kinds of thoughts she had that were stimulating worry rather than peace. Along the way, we delved into the perspectives I offered in the earlier chapters of this book, which resonated with spiritual beliefs she already held. They gave her a foundation from which she could choose more peaceful perspectives. She stayed committed to getting her boat out of the stream moving away from her natural desires and into the one flowing toward them.

I am not exaggerating when I say her life has completely transformed. She is now living a relaxed, happy, and deeply satisfying life, one in which desires emerge naturally and she follows their energy. All her family relationships have improved without the constricting energy of worry interfering with her natural enjoyment of those she loves. She has released old fears and resentments and is living peacefully in the Now, trusting in the goodness of Life. And she is a joy to be around.

Jessica is a living and breathing example of how powerful knowing how you want to *feel* really is. She didn't know "what" she wanted when we first started working together. But in her commitment to shifting from worry to peace, she discovered greater pleasure in the life she was living. She also learned to say *yes* to new things and experiences she discovered she wanted—things she might not have allowed herself to consider before—and found great satisfaction in them.

Jessica is now in the flow of her own beautiful life, without having made a big deal about figuring out what she wants. Instead, she focuses on her desire to feel at peace, and all good things come from that. She has also made a habit of the next suggestion I offer to those who don't know exactly what they want:

Acknowledge and honor your preferences, moment to moment.

As I said earlier, no desire is too small to matter or too large to embrace. As you learn to recognize and honor the seemingly small ones, you establish the importance of desire in your Local Self consciousness, and you cultivate a deeper sense of worthiness. These vibrational shifts make it easier for more of your desires to become known to you.

If you're like most people, you may have become habituated to doing the same or similar things, with the same people, under predictable circumstances. This practice requires that you take a brief inner moment, before you move into the next activity or make a choice about something, to check in with yourself to see what you would prefer in that moment.

If you can honor your preference with little resistance or worry, do so. If not, simply take note of your genuine preferences and observe them over time. Let them reveal to you what you might genuinely want, or not want, in your life. If they reveal what feels like a big, impossible, or impractical desire, just note your fearful thoughts and don't force yourself into any action. There's no need to jump off a cliff, hoping against all odds you can learn to fly. You can learn to fly and *then* jump off the cliff.

Or more accurately, you can learn to fly, create some momentum toward what you want and just *fly*. No cliff required.

My decision to stop taking continuing professional education courses is a good example of honoring a genuine preference, one I learned in hindsight was a helpful and loving step on a guided journey toward what I truly wanted. It felt a little risky but not hugely so. In fact, it felt more liberating than risky, which was an indicator that it was a good choice for me.

So, turn up the dial of your self-awareness and begin noticing your genuine desires and preferences, moment to moment. Act on the ones you feel comfortable acting on and give yourself the gift of reflecting on all of them. Open to One Source for further insights or guidance about them.

Follow only guidance that feels good or right in some way. Ideas that feel scary or risky or urgent aren't coming from One Source. They're coming from fear. We'll go into this in greater depth in future chapters. For now, just be curious about your preferences and desires and honor as many of them as you can.

My third suggestion to those of you who don't know what you want is this:

Admit what your heart of hearts already knows.

What I call the "heart of hearts" is the connection between our Local Self and One Source. I sometimes think of it as a portal through which the love and wisdom of One Source flows into my awareness. Often, when clients tell me they don't know what they want, what's true is that they *do* know, in their heart of hearts, but they've already dismissed it in their minds as impossible, impractical, unimportant, or selfish.

Now is the time to set those judgments aside. You may want to reread chapter one to connect with the deeper truth of how vital and important your desires really are. Then relax, get quiet and go within. What, in your heart of hearts, have you longed to be, do, or have? What lights you up? What would you love to experience more of in your life right now? What might you want to create, to explore or to learn?

Don't try to force an answer, or to figure it out analytically. Remember, desire arises from the heart. And remember, too, that you have many desires, of all shapes and sizes. This is not an attempt to find that one big desire that will change your life. It is an opportunity to relax, quiet your mind, and admit to yourself what your heart of hearts already knows.

And then to say *yes*.

Getting to *yes*

If, in this moment, you're still not clear about what you really want, relax. Keep focusing on how you want to feel, honoring your desires and preferences in as many moments as you can, and spending quality time with yourself in an open, receptive state so you can connect with your heart of hearts.

Remember that *what you want wants you*. It is pulsing with the very force of Life itself toward realization, finding as many ways as it can to get your attention. Let it do the work. Your job is to feel as good as you can feel and trust that you will easily recognize your genuine desires. When you do, give yourself some time to appreciate how good a pure desire *feels* when you acknowledge it. Don't force yourself into action, but act on any related ideas or impulses that feel good to you.

It is often helpful to identify or articulate your desire in a way that inspires you but doesn't introduce resistance. Your translation of a desire into an idea is often the first step in cultivating a consciousness that allows it to manifest.

Finding the "perfect words" is not necessary. Desires don't require precise definitions before they can be realized. They only require your vibrational harmony with them. All that's needed is for you to learn to cultivate that harmony, which we'll continue to explore in depth throughout this book.

I offer the suggestion to articulate your desires in a way that inspires you but doesn't introduce resistance because I've found it can be helpful in two ways: it can help you better recognize your desires and develop trust that they can be realized. Let's take a closer look at this idea.

From heart to mind: be clear but not overly specific

A genuine desire is, by its very nature, inspiring. It is uplifting. Yet sometimes, as our minds translate the desire into language, our habitual ways of thinking creep in and the essence of the desire gets lost or diminished in translation. If the desire you've acknowledged doesn't inspire you, or it if immediately generates resistance in the form of uncomfortable feelings, something essential was lost or something unnecessary was added.

Let's look first at resistance, because I've observed that it is more common for people to resist their desires than to be uninspired by them. The most common form of resistance is doubt or disbelief: you may have already convinced yourself that what you want isn't practical or achievable, or that you don't have what it takes to realize it.

Another common form of resistance can arise if you turn your desire into a goal and put it on a timetable for realization. This can introduce rigidity, anxiety or even fear into the experience, because a specific goal can become something you judge yourself unfavorably against if you don't reach it "fast enough" or manifest every detail you identified as being part of it.

These types of resistance tend to arise when desires are defined very specifically or in grandiose terms, relative to your current experience. On the other hand, desires that are very general can feel uninspiring. Their lack of specificity can lead to a lack of focus, perhaps even confusion. A certain degree of specificity provides a sense of direction and purpose that can help you stay connected to your true inspiration.

The simple guideline I offer my clients—in the articulation of desires in a way that inspires them but doesn't introduce resistance—is to identify desires that are *clear but not overly specific*.

Moving from general to specific

Let's say that you feel mostly unhappy in your life. You're not fulfilled in your work, you squabble with your partner over just about everything, and you weigh twenty pounds more than you'd like to weigh. You have a desire to be happy, which is completely natural. Your desire is calling you toward the quality of life you are innately deserving of.

Yet "happy" may seem vague and out of reach to you, so identifying your desire as simply the desire to be happy may not be specific enough to help you feel that it's realizable. So, you begin to explore how "happy" might look and feel in certain areas or circumstances in your life. For example, you might recognize that you want to

Feel more fulfilled in your work.

Be at peace with your partner.

Feel energized in your body.

As you continue to explore this further, you might further recognize that you want to

Do work that fully utilizes your marketing skills and gives you opportunities to learn more, which excites you.

Be able to be in conversations with your partner without feeling defensive.

Start running on a regular basis, which you once loved.

As you continue focusing on your more specific desires in this exploratory way, you notice that your desires feel more real, and more realizable. In particular, the idea of running feels not just doable, but inviting. You can sense that giving yourself the gift of running will help you feel better not only physically, but mentally and emotionally as well. You feel excited by it and more than willing to get started. And so, in a peaceful moment of clarity about how you feel, you say *yes* to that desire.

In this example, your exploration of the more specific ways you could feel happy helped you to identify a desire that is clear and focused enough to inspire a *yes*, without feelings of doubt or resignation. Note that process itself is not an analytical one.

It isn't about making lists of pros and cons to see which desire has the longest "pro" list or the shortest "con" list. It isn't about doing a time management study to estimate whether it would be easier to fit running or a job search into your schedule. It isn't about assessing your successes and failures from past attempts at making improvements in those areas of your life, to figure out which one would be best to try now.

It is about lovingly exploring your feelings and noticing where you can most strongly sense the energy of desire in this fresh moment of Now.

From specific to general

Now imagine a different scenario. You're in a corporate job that isn't a good fit for your talents, desires, and skills. Having had lots of training in goal setting, with an emphasis on setting big goals, you let your imagination run wild and come up with what feels like an ideal job: director of finance at XYZ Corporation. Believing that a goal without a timetable is a goal that will never be reached, you daringly challenge yourself to reach that goal within a year.

Your initial excitement about the goal soon gives way to doubt and frustration as you contemplate the many connections you'll need to make with people who work at that company, the luck you'll have to have in order for that position to be open within a year, the skills you'll need to develop, the experience you'll need to qualify you for that kind of position, and on and on, in order to reach it. You realize it might not even be possible. So now instead of feeling excited, you feel defeated.

It's time to step back to the more general level of experience from which your desire arose. What you want is to find a job that fully utilizes your talents and skills, and the opportunity to grow into more of the kind of work you desire. That's very clear but not overly specific in terms of company, job title or timetable. Those explicitly defined elements were the very things that generated doubt and frustration–resistance–when you turned your desire into a goal.

As you reflect on this more generally stated desire, you recognize there are probably countless jobs that match it. Finding one is more than just possible; it feels probable and maybe even likely or inevitable. This is an easy desire to which you can say *yes*.

Knowing how you feel is where the magic is

Both scenarios could have been written very differently to illustrate other nuances on the journey of realizing desires. For example, in the second scenario, you could have been feeling satisfied in your job yet aware that you long for something more enlivening. Having developed habits of connection with One Source, you might have received an intuitive vision of yourself as the director of finance at XYZ Corporation by the end of the year. You might have been inspired by that vision and felt an inner knowing that it would come to fruition. And assuming you kept your Local Self thoughts and beliefs in harmony with it, it would.

We'll be visiting many examples of the manifestation process as the remaining chapters unfold. What I want to emphasize here are three important things to know about feelings:

When you're generally feeling good in your life—peaceful, trusting, optimistic—the ideas you have and the intuitive flashes you receive are likely coming from One Source.

When you're generally not feeling good in your life—perhaps frustrated, resigned, or depressed—the thoughts you frequently entertain are likely not coming from One Source.

Knowing how you feel now, and how you want to feel, provides the sense of direction that will help you shift your thoughts into harmony with your desires.

Take a moment now to get quiet, connect with your heart of hearts, and give yourself permission to acknowledge any desires currently pulsing there, then reflect on this chapter's Reflection Point:

Reflection Point

What I want, wants me. My desires already exist in the eternal Now, ready to be expressed. They become my life experience when my thoughts are in harmony with them.

6

DESIRE IMPOSTERS

Give yourself permission to want what you really want.

My career was zigging and zagging. After having liberated myself from taking continuing professional education courses to maintain my status as a CPA, my longing to do work I truly loved was emboldened. It was as persistent in getting my attention as I was fearful to entertain it, and I wobbled between saying a tentative *yes* to saying a resigned *no* to it, again and again.

Over the course of about ten years, I left and returned to the corporate world three times. During that period, I opened and closed a holistic healing center, then later attempted to establish myself as an energy healer at another center. On each return to the corporate world, I took on a different role, hoping each time that the new position would work for me. It never did.

During my transition from corporate employee to teacher and writer, I fell prey to virtually all the desire imposters I will introduce in this chapter. But before I go on, I want to be extremely clear about something: desire imposters are not bad or wrong. I was not *wrong* for having pursued them, and you are not wrong for having pursued them, either, if you have.

As I am often reminded in times of deep inner connection, there is no right or wrong. There are only experience, learning, and growth—

occurring through countless people in countless ways as we awaken to more and more of who we are.

The bumps and wobbles I experienced in my career transition showed me that every time I experienced something unwanted, my desire for work that I loved intensified. That's how I learned that desire always turns us toward One Source—toward fulfillment. Although I repeatedly turned away from my genuine desire rather than toward it, desire always called me back.

Still, I wanted an easier path. My ever-deepening interest in energy, consciousness, and spirituality had led me to teachers who claimed we could grow through joy as well as through pain, and I wanted to learn more about the path of joy. Growing through joy is what I now think of as letting our genuine desires lead us into more and more of who we really are.

This is simple in concept but more challenging in execution. Given the confusing and often contradictory messages we've received about desire, it's easy to convince ourselves we want things we don't really want, or to be convinced by others. These things are what I'm calling desire imposters.

How could any desire be an imposter?

In the last chapter I defined what I call pure or genuine desires as our *desires to create, to express, to experience, and to share.* They are the impulses of Love wanting to experience itself through our individual and brilliantly unique combinations of Divine intelligences, talents, proclivities, preferences, and passions. Genuine desires, which are frequencies of pure energy pulsing wordlessly in the eternal Now, enter the Trinity of Creation when we translate them into an idea.

What I call desire imposters are ideas arising from a different source. They arise from false beliefs about who we are, who others are, and what is possible to create in our lives. In contrast with a pure desire's intention for expressing the fullness of who we are, the underlying intention of desire imposters is to *prove* ourselves in some way or to avoid something unwanted. These desire imposters arise not from our fullness but from our perceived sense of lack.

The hallmark of a desire imposter is that it's something we've figured out solely in our heads, often in reaction to something painful. The loving guidance of the heart is usually all but ignored. In my career transition, I repeatedly tried to *figure out* my next steps—which I desperately wanted to figure out because I was so unhappy—based on assessment, analysis, or persuasive arguments. I didn't consult my heart of hearts, where the longing to teach and write waited patiently for me to fully acknowledge it.

I didn't consult my heart of hearts because I had already deemed the longing within it to be impractical. The shutting down of my own desire reflected my false belief in separation from One Source—and therefore from the innate brilliance, creativity, joy, and abundance of One Source. I didn't see myself as a magnificent expression of that One Source, pulsing with my own unique combination of Divine Intelligences, talents, passions, and proclivities, and fully worthy of living an abundant and creatively fulfilled life. Far from it.

I saw myself as an individual who needed to prove her *worthiness* to have a good life by working hard and competing with others for the scarce resources and rewards that were available. I understood that I had a certain type of intelligence and skill that could help me compete and I was motivated by fear—fear of not being approved of and fear of not having enough money—to win. I was in full-blown separation consciousness and because of that, I only had access to certain types of thoughts.

Here are examples of things I believed at the time that kept pushing me to pursue things I didn't really want:

I need to work hard to make a living. Work isn't supposed to be fun.

I don't have another choice. I tried a career in healing, and it failed. This is what I'm educated and trained to do, and I've already invested years in this career. I've got to make it work.

If I make enough money now, I can retire early and then enjoy my life.

This is not an exhaustive list, but I include it here to help illustrate the link between separation consciousness—believing we are separate from the creativity, abundance, and brilliance of One Source—and desire imposters. They go hand in hand. Because I believed these things, I kept trying to convince myself that I wanted what I didn't really want.

I've worked with countless clients and students over the years who, like me, have tried to figure out what they want, or what they "should" be doing with their lives, almost solely in their heads. And like me, they were driven by an uncomfortable emotion—perhaps fear, anger, worry or guilt, brought on by their false and limiting beliefs. While there are myriad patterns of belief that give rise to desire imposters, I've observed five of them that are quite common, especially among those on a spiritual path:

> What others think you should want
>
> What you think others want or need
>
> The Service Trap
>
> The One Big Thing
>
> The Sensible Alternative

As I offer my perspective on desire imposters, and the distinctions between them and genuine desires, please hold the labels lightly. I only offer them to help you recognize distinctions that could be beneficial to you. They are not meant to become labels you attach to yourself.

What others think you should want

Given the prevalent messages that are strenuously offered from the media, religious institutions, groups, colleagues, friends, and family—messages about how we're supposed to look, feel, think, and live our lives—it's easy for even the most clear-minded among us to be convinced about the "rightness" of certain pursuits, and then to further convince ourselves that we want to pursue them.

That was certainly true of me. I had convinced myself, based on strong input from my father and others whose opinions I respected, that a high-paying corporate career was what I should pursue. Even though I knew there were countless happy people outside the corporate world who were financially stable and even very wealthy, I didn't see myself as having what it would take to create a life like that. So, I kept trying to convince myself that my unfulfilling corporate work was somehow right for me.

If you are continually dissatisfied with whatever you're pursuing, it likely means one of three things:

Yours is a genuine desire, but you've got so many beliefs that aren't in harmony with it that the desire can't flow into your experience.

Yours is a genuine desire, but you've defined it so specifically that you've made it harder for yourself to believe it's possible.

It isn't a genuine desire. It is something you have convinced yourself you *should* do.

If you recognize that either of the *genuine* desire descriptions is true for you, know that we will continue to explore how to bring our thoughts into harmony with our genuine desires throughout this book. And if it isn't a genuine desire, rest assured that the simple act of acknowledging that you don't genuinely desire whatever you are pursuing is liberating. It creates space into which your genuine desires can flow into your awareness. Invite your desires to make themselves known to you by asking, "What might I genuinely want to create or experience now?"

If you're not sure whether you *genuinely* want what you're currently pursuing, let me suggest something simple and direct to help you get clear: ask yourself *why* you want what you're currently pursuing.

Genuine desires are all about self-expression; they reflect our desires to create, express, experience, and share. Desire imposters are all about proving ourselves or avoiding something unwanted.

Is it possible for a given pursuit to be both a genuine desire and a desire imposter? Yes. Or more accurately, it's possible for us to interfere with the natural flow of genuine desire into our lives with thoughts about having to prove ourselves or avoid something unwanted.

For example, my desire to write books has been tangled up for years in painful and limiting beliefs about the kind of book it "should" be, my sense of my unworthiness to write it, and fears about what its possible failure might reveal about me. I had to finally get to the pure place of acknowledging that I am a teacher and a writer, and I long to write books, and *let that be fully enough*.

If you sense that you've tangled your genuine desire for something with similarly unhelpful thoughts, focus on the essence of the desire itself and say a simple *yes* to it. Yes, this is what I want. Stay with the purity of the desire for as long as you can, breathing deeply to give it space within you to grow.

What you think others need or want

I sometimes think of this desire imposter as sneaky. It's related to what I call the Service Trap, which we'll look at next, but I wanted to highlight it as a distinct imposter because it's more subtle and therefore easy to miss. It's also very common.

This is the habit of making choices based on what you think others in your life want or need, with virtually no regard for your own desires, requirements, and preferences. It arises not from generosity, but from a belief that your desires are less important than theirs.

I've observed that parents, particularly mothers, often fall prey to this imposter. They believe that the wants and needs of their children are always more important than their own. The sneaky elements of this desire im-poster are revealed in the words "always" and "more."

Everyone's desires are equally important because everyone is a unique ex-pression of One Source. And our desires come in all shapes and sizes, from simple preferences to lifelong passions. No desire is too small to matter or too big to embrace. All desires are important because all desires are the im-pulse of Love to express itself, in countless ways and through countless people.

There are such things, of course, as timing and intensity. For example, you may desire a warm bath when, suddenly, your eleven-year-old son comes home early from a neighborhood softball game with a bloody nose. In that moment you would honor his desire and need for comfort and heal-ing rather than your desire to be in the tub. In another moment, however, you might ask your partner to tend to your child so you can honor your desire for a warm bath.

There is a distinction between thinking that other people's needs and de-sires are *always more important* than your own and understanding that all needs and desires are important—including your own—yet being able to make wise and loving choices in any moment.

A belief that other people's needs and desires are always more important than your own can only arise in separation consciousness, which reflects a perception of yourself and others as separate from the all-loving, all-knowing, and all-powerful One Source. If you see yourself as smaller and more vulnerable than others, you may conclude that you are less im-portant than they are. You aren't, of course, because you are an expression of the same powerful One Source as they are. But in the false belief that you are, you may presume that your desires aren't important, either. And you might also come to believe that, by focusing on fulfilling others' needs and desires, you're at least doing something worthwhile.

If you see yourself as bigger and more powerful than others, who seem frail or vulnerable to you, you may conclude that you are responsible for their well-being. You aren't, of course, because they are expressions of the same powerful One Source as you are. But in your belief that you're responsible for them, you may believe that it's your job to make them happy.

I'm not saying you should stop doing the helpful and supportive things you're doing for others (although you may choose to do less of some things and to do others differently). I'm drawing a distinction here between the *quality of experience* we have when we're in harmony with One Source and when we're not, even if the actions are the same.

When we are in harmony with One Source, we know that we are worthy of living a fulfilled life. We trust in the natural unfolding of our desires and appreciate the process of it. We enjoy sharing our gifts with others. We see opportunities to be helpful and we delight in offering our help, because we are naturally generous when we're in harmony with One Source. We follow our inner guidance about who, how, and when to help, knowing that Divine Intelligence orchestrates the highest and best outcomes.

When we are in harmony with One Source, we see others as expressions of that same One Source, worthy of living a fulfilled life. We understand that if they are in painful circumstances, it is fundamentally because they have not fully realized their magnificence—their creativity, brilliance, and power—and that the same is true for us, in our moments of pain. We help them out of a genuine desire to support who they are becoming.

As an example, imagine you have a daughter who is currently having a difficult time with one subject in school, and she is losing confidence in herself. You worry about her. Your worry is an indicator that you're not in harmony with One Source, who sees your daughter's brilliance and understands the joy she'll experience as she wakes up to more and more of it.

Her birthday is coming up and, feeling responsible for her happiness, you go out of your way to plan the best celebration ever. You work on the planning late at night, after she's asleep, so it will be a surprise. You fret over the details and hope you're making the right choices. You feel increasingly anxious as the day approaches and hope everything goes well.

The day finally arrives, and you're wound up tight. You watch your daughter closely throughout the party, trying to figure out if she's enjoying herself. You really can't tell. You barely touch your food and don't let yourself begin to relax until after the party is over. You think it went all right but you're still not sure. You drop into bed that night, exhausted.

This is obviously an example of pursuing a desire to make your daughter happy. It's perfectly natural, of course, for us to want our loved ones to be happy. What makes this a desire imposter is that it arises from fear and worry rather than from trust and generosity. Those emotions indicate that you're not in harmony with One Source, which means that the wisdom and guidance of One Source aren't available to you.

Now imagine that you've found ways of staying in harmony with One Source most of the time. When your daughter confides in you that she's worried about possibly failing one of her courses in school, you reassure her that she is loved no matter what, and that this is an opportunity for *her* to learn to love herself through the challenge rather than berate herself.

As her birthday approaches, you feel excited about the opportunity to celebrate her brilliance. Coming out of meditation one morning, you have an inspired idea for a party that you know will delight her. The idea delights you, too, and you jump into the planning of the event with gusto. You want it to be a surprise, so you do as much of the planning as you can after she's asleep. Keeping it a secret adds an element of fun for you.

On the day of the party, you're bursting with excitement as you anticipate her reaction to the surprise. Sure enough, she is thrilled and proceeds to enjoy herself thoroughly on her special day. You do, too, appreciating how all the elements you planned came together in such a delightful way. You feel good about having followed your intuitive guidance to host the party and go to bed feeling very satisfied.

In these two examples the actions are almost identical, yet the quality of experience in the second is far more satisfying than in the first, because in the latter you are in harmony with One Source most of the time. You aren't trying to "make" her happy; you are celebrating all that is wonderful about her.

The deeper truth is that we cannot "make" others happy. We can inspire and support them toward their happiness when we are consistently in harmony with One Source, and that harmony naturally includes the fulfillment of our own important desires.

If this desire imposter feels familiar to you, give yourself some time to reflect on your own personal desires—perhaps for greater peace of mind, more time to yourself, more fun in your life, a sense of balance, or whatever your heart of hearts is quietly calling you toward. Say a simple *yes* to your desires. Yes, this is what I want. Stay with the purity of the desire for as long as you can, breathing deeply to give it space within you to grow.

The Service Trap

The Service Trap is similar to the previous desire imposter because the focus remains almost exclusively on others, with little regard to personal desires and preferences. In this case, however, the others aren't loved ones, but people in the world who you believe are in need.

This imposter is particularly common among spiritually minded people, perhaps because of the importance that has long been placed in many spiritual traditions on selfless service. It is the belief that you should be of service in some meaningful way to fulfill the needs of others. The key word that reveals this desire as an imposter is "should."

In the flow of Life, giving to others who want or need what we can give is the most natural thing in the world. It is a genuine desire arising from the creativity and generosity of One Source. There is inherent balance, symmetry, and harmony in the diversity of our Divine expression. What we genuinely desire to create and share is exactly what others will greatly benefit from receiving. We are the answer to their prayers, just as many others have been the answer to ours.

What distinguishes the Service Trap from the natural flow of giving and receiving is the underlying impetus for action. One is a feeling of guilt or obligation, and the other is an impulse to be generous or creative. And as is the case with the previous desire imposter, the quality of experience between the two is vastly different.

I worked briefly with a client several years ago, whom I'll call Bob, who was recently retired. He felt adrift without the structure and focus of his job, as if his life no longer had meaning or purpose. He associated purpose with being of service, and he was trying hard to figure out how to be of service in a meaningful way.

Like others with whom I've worked who weren't connected with their genuine desires, he was trying to figure out an answer through analysis. Having identified various groups of disadvantaged people who had specific needs, he wanted to find the neediest group that might benefit from his specific skills.

When I asked him which skills he most enjoyed using, and how he genuinely wanted to give of himself, he didn't fully understand my questions. He believed his own preferences were irrelevant to the decision.

I explained to Bob that when genuine desire is missing, we're not in harmony with One Source. And when we're not in harmony with One Source, we are giving far less than we have the capacity to give. I helped him understand that our genuine desires are the very pulse of Love moving through us as Life. What could be more generous than Life itself?

I also encouraged him to consider the *energies* of guilt and obligation. They are heavy, damning, and rigid. Those frequencies are not at all in harmony with the energy of desire, which is expansive, generous, and life-giving. Would Bob rather receive something from someone who gives it to

101

him out of a sense of guilt and obligation, or out of a sense of love and appreciation?

I'll never forget the look on his face when the realization hit home: his genuine desires were neither selfish nor irrelevant. They were his path of greatest generosity and fulfillment.

Bob was able to let go of thinking he should utilize his organizational skills to coordinate the collection and distribution of goods to people who had recently lost their homes in a hurricane, which up to that point had been the choice toward which he was leaning. He admitted that he hated organizing things, even though he had the ability to do it. Instead, he decided to volunteer for a literacy program that helped children learn to read and write, which were two passions of his.

In making his choice, Bob felt uplifted. He grasped the inspired truth in what Howard Thurman wrote: "Don't ask what the world needs. Ask what makes you come alive and go do it. Because what the world needs is people who have come alive."

In contrast to coming alive, falling into the Service Trap leaves you feeling exhausted because you're trying so hard to figure out how you're "supposed" to be of service. It can also leave you feeling guilty and undeserving of the good in your life, which is the opposite of what One Source wants for you.

If this desire imposter feels familiar to you, remember that when you are in harmony with One Source, you are naturally creative and giving. You don't need to force yourself to do something for others; what you want to create and share benefits those who are open to receive it. And you are an open channel for fresh inspiration about new things to create and share.

Remember, too, that no one's desires are more or less important than your own, and that it isn't your job to figure out how everyone's needs will be met. It's your job to figure out how to stay connected with One Source, and to trust its incredible intelligence to orchestrate the giving and receiving of gifts in a way that uplifts everyone.

The One Big Thing

Much has been written about people who have either a sweeping, singular talent or a sweeping, singular vision, or both, and how they have changed the world. From the musical genius of Mozart to the uncompromising commitment to personal expression of Martha Graham, from the clear-minded vision of freedom through peaceful means of Gandhi to the bold vision of John F. Kennedy, who declared in 1961 that we would put a man on the moon by the end of the decade, our minds and hearts have been opened by countless individuals to a greater sense of possibility, and a deepened appreciation for the power of the human spirit to create new worlds.

To feel inspired is perhaps one of the most exhilarating and empowered feelings we can have. Yet comparing ourselves to those who have inspired us and finding ourselves lacking is one of the most damaging things we can do to our possibilities for personal accomplishment and fulfillment.

I've worked with many people who have done just that. They've come to believe that the only contributions that really matter are the ones that are seen and felt by large numbers of people. And they see themselves lacking the kind of talent or boldness of vision that can generate such a contribution.

Sometimes they have a talent they would love to nurture, but because they can't see how it could grow into something "big," they try to figure out something else instead. A common approach here is an attempt to create a plan for what I call the conglomerate: a job or career or activity that utilizes as many of their talents, skills, and passions as possible. Another is to relegate the talent to hobby status and figure out some other way of combining skills and experience into something that's seemingly big or important.

Regardless of how they respond to the false beliefs that only "big" contributions matter, and that they need to find a way to make such a contribution, the results are the same. They feel inadequate and without purpose, or they're exhausted and frustrated from trying too hard to figure out what their calling is. Inadequacy, exhaustion, and frustration are indicators of not being in harmony with One Source.

If this feels familiar to you, let me assure you that your desires, of all shapes and sizes, *are* your calling. They are calling you to focus on them, to bring yourself into harmony with them and allow them to flow into your experience. Your unique talents, proclivities, and preferences are a gift to the world that only you can give. You're not supposed to live a life like anyone else; you came here to live *your* beautiful life.

The Sensible Alternative

This desire imposter is essentially the "version" of our desire that our analytical minds have deemed practical.

For example, I may have musical talent and dream of a career as a performing musician, but I've already convinced myself that could never happen, so I decide to become a church organist instead. My choice to become a church organist might have arisen from a genuine desire to share my music in a way that feels good to me. But in this example, I have talked myself into believing that my talent is very limited, and this option—which doesn't light me up—is the only viable one available to me.

In general, the Sensible Alternative imposter arises from either a self-critical tendency we have developed with respect to our talents, or a strong belief that we could never 'make a living" doing what we love to do, or both.

We *never* benefit ourselves or the world by dismissing or diminishing our talent. That kind of thinking simply must be seen for what it is— unhelpful and untrue—and a commitment made to learn how to nurture our talents.

Similarly, we never benefit ourselves by demanding that any talent we desire to cultivate must be the primary channel through which financial abundance flows to us. There are countless channels through which abundance can flow to us. Some of them may be directly related to a specific talent we have, others may not.

When we decide that our talents are only worth pursuing if we can see a way for them to generate income, we cut ourselves off from the pulse of Life that wants to flow through us as we nurture those talents. As we cut ourselves off from the flow of Life, we cut ourselves off from our creativity, our joy, and our genius. And we cut ourselves off from the inner prompts and outer synchronicities that otherwise guide us, step by step, toward our greatest fulfillment.

Saying *yes* to our desires as a path of awakening to who we really are is an *orientation* to Life, one that is vastly different from setting specific, data-based goals and using our analytical minds to figure out how to reach them. It is about flowing *with* Life and trusting that we are worthy of being supported on all levels, including financial, as we follow our desires into self-expression.

It is also about trusting the infinite intelligence and creativity of One Source to guide us toward the opportunities that become channels through which abundance can flow here in the physical dimension. Developing this trust is a key element of bringing our Local Self consciousness into unity consciousness, which is in harmony with our desires.

You have nothing to prove

Desire imposters, in all their myriad disguises, are things we have convinced ourselves we want when we are in separation consciousness. Not understanding our worthiness, our brilliance, and our creative power as extensions of One Source, we buy into the false premises of unworthiness and scarcity that are the hallmarks of separation consciousness. We don't trust in a loving intelligence that wants us to succeed and be happy; we think we must figure out how to leverage our talents and skills to compete successfully for the things we need, or to prove our worthiness, or both. Then we try to convince ourselves that we want to do those things.

And yet our genuine desires, pulsing with the creative power of Life itself that will lead to our fulfillment, are ever ready for our recognition, our acknowledgment, and our embrace. They are ready, *now*, for our *yes*.

Take a moment now to pause and reflect on this chapter's Reflection Point:

Reflection Point

As an extension of One Source, which is Love, I have nothing to fix or prove. I have the glorious opportunity to express more and more of who I really am.

7

YOUR THOUGHTS, YOUR WORLD

Become a connoisseur of loving thoughts.

It was New Year's Day, and I was rereading my journal entries from the year just passed, in preparation for setting intentions for the new year. One of my strongest desires at that time was for my work to expand and my business to thrive. As I closed my journal after reviewing the final entry, I felt *stunned*. How could I not have recognized earlier what was now so crystal clear? It was no wonder my business was not yet thriving. Page after page of the journal was filled with statements of crippling doubt, runaway worry and, often, damning self-criticism. Nothing could have thrived in such a hostile environment.

That was when I began to understand that my job wasn't to build a business. My job was to create a safe inner space in which my desires for a thriving business could grow and flourish. Self-judgment could not be allowed in that safe inner space. I vowed then and there to learn how to love myself into a life I loved.

The safe space I promised to create is what I now refer to as a consciousness of genuine Self Love. It is the expression of unity consciousness at the level of the individual. In unity consciousness, we understand ourselves to be individual expressions of One Source, which is Love, so I capitalize Self Love to indicate this profound truth of our identity.

I had to learn how to cultivate a consciousness of genuine Self Love. I had to learn more about the relational dynamic between thought and manifestation so I could work within it. I had to practice bringing my thoughts into harmony with my desires, little by little and moment by moment. I literally had to change the *way* I was thinking.

Over the years I've learned quite a lot about what that takes. I'm still learning, of course, but in this chapter, I'll share insights I've gained that have helped my clients and me better understand how beliefs are formed and, therefore, how to shift them.

Recalling the big picture

To begin, remember that your consciousness—essentially the way you think—is the vibrational layer through which your desires flow from the nonphysical in your eternal Now, into your physical experience in the here and now. Manifestation is all about vibrational resonance: as we bring our Local Self thoughts into vibrational harmony with our desires, our desires become our lived experience.

Because every thought that has ever been held still exists in the mass consciousness of humanity, the nature, variety, and specificity of thoughts with which we can resonate is vast beyond description. As individuals with free will, we can choose to cultivate a Local Self consciousness that is in harmony with what we *want*, rather than in harmony with what is vibrating in mass consciousness.

This is true even if many or even most people are vibrating, and therefore creating experiences, in ways we do not want. Remember, the collective consciousness, and therefore experience, of humanity is just that—a collective. It is a collective of individual consciousnesses and individual experiences. *Creative power exists at the level of the individual.*

Because we have individual free will, we have the freedom to focus our attention on what we want and the freedom to choose what we believe. This cannot be overemphasized.

We are not sharing a singular reality that is happening to us, regardless of our personal desires and preferences. We are creating individual realities that intersect and combine to form a shared reality.

I emphasize this point because it is in the observation of "reality"—the shared reality of humanity—that we often lose sight of ourselves as individual expressions of One Source, with the freedom and ability to create lives we love. We often conclude that the more people who experience something, the more real and inevitable it must be. Increasing the vibrational strength of this "something" does increase the probability that more people will experience it. But that does not have to be the case for any of us, individually. If we conclude that it does, however, then it becomes true for us. Our personal conclusions become beliefs in our Local Self consciousness.

Even so, this can be shifted, starting Now. Our individual free will grants each of us the ability to manifest our desires through the freedom we have to bring our personal thoughts into harmony with our desires, regardless of what others are doing.

Exercising that ability takes some practice. In chapter five, I offered the metaphor of the two streams of thought—one flowing toward what we want and one flowing away from it. I suggested that the effort required to get out of one stream and into another is immensely worthwhile.

The nature of this effort is not one of struggle. (Struggle is an indicator that you're pushing against your own desires.) It is one of honoring a commitment to love yourself forward and experimenting with ways to do that which feel good and helpful to you. So, at its core, it's a consistency of focus on feeling good.

To recap the Big Picture, you are a uniquely brilliant expression of the all-knowing, all-powerful, and all-loving One Source. Your desires are the desires of One Source to express and experience itself through you, as you. You are a vibrational being, and your desires manifest into physical experience through the vibrational harmony of your Local Self consciousness with them. You have free will. Therefore, you can bring your Local Self consciousness into harmony with your desires, regardless of what others are doing. Let's take a closer look at the nuances and dynamics of this process.

Only active thoughts have creative power

As a vibrational being, the tone or quality of your consciousness determines the tone or quality of your life, and it sets the stage for the specific opportunities, circumstances, and relationships you experience. It determines the kinds of ideas you have, the types of people who show up in your life, the nature of opportunities that present themselves to you and so much more, because the powerful Law of Attraction is bringing to you that which resonates—vibrates on a harmonic frequency—with your thoughts.

As you vibrate, so you create.

Remember that when I use the word "thought," I'm including all types of mental constructs in your Local Self consciousness: assumptions, conclusions, images, memories, projections, and so on. The thoughts with sufficient vibrational power to yield manifestations can be considered *active thoughts*. Active thoughts fall into two categories:

> Thoughts you're focusing on now.

> Thoughts you've already *accepted as true*, which are beliefs, regardless of whether you're currently focusing on them and *regardless of whether they are in harmony with what you want.*

We'll take a close look at the first category throughout the remainder of the book, as we continue to explore how to cultivate thought patterns that support our desires. Let's now consider the second category, because thoughts in this category can easily give rise to manifestations we don't understand, which leads many people to conclude that the Law of Attraction isn't working for them. The Law of Attraction is always working, yet in many cases our understanding of it is incomplete.

Imagine you are the mother of three young children, and you also have a full-time job. Your children are the top priority in your life. You're not thinking, "My children are my top priority," all day, every day. When you're at work, you're focused on what you're doing. But if your boss asks you to go on an extended out-of-town assignment, that thought likely comes immediately into your awareness.

Consider now the uncountable number of thoughts you have—things you believe to be true about yourself and about life—that are in your consciousness. You don't think of them every day or even most days, but depending on their strength, they have the power to draw situations to you that relate to them.

There are many avenues through which you can come to accept something as true, such as the beliefs your parents held, religious teachings, strong views held by people or groups you resonate with, and conclusions drawn from scientific and other kinds of research. Perhaps the clearest and strongest avenue through which you come to accept things as true is your observation of manifested physical reality—yours and others.

For example, if many people in your life dislike their jobs yet feel they have no choice but to stay in them, you observe how common the experience is and conclude that work is not supposed to be enjoyable, and that one must simply endure a job because it's the only way to make money. It doesn't seem to be a belief; it appears to be the reality. This is incredibly common, and it is why I drew your attention to this dynamic in the previous section. Remember, just because something has manifested, even for a lot of people, it doesn't mean the manifestation of it is inevitable for you. But if you conclude that it is, then your conclusion—your belief—can make it true for you.

There are other means through which you can accept thoughts as true. A significant yet often unrecognized one is mass consciousness, itself (as opposed to observed physical realities) and the vibrational thoughtforms within it that are active. Because of the powerful Law of Attraction, thoughts that are accepted as true in mass consciousness continue to increase in strength and stability as more people focus on them. For example, the thought of unworthiness is vibrating strongly in human consciousness right now because we are dominantly in separation consciousness, which is the only consciousness from which the concept of unworthiness can arise.

You may never have thought of yourself as unworthy, but if you've recently had a loss of confidence due to mistakes you feel you've made, you could be in the vibrational vicinity of the thoughtform of unworthiness. If so, the Law of Attraction will bring that thought to you. You might then conclude that you are unworthy of the good that Life has to offer.

At the other end of the spectrum, a wonderful avenue through which thoughts can come into your awareness is your Expanded Self. Your Expanded Self is the part of you that has remained nonphysical, even as "you"—at the Local Self level—live in this physical dimension. Your Expanded Self is a distinct expression of One Source which sees and knows you as a further expression of that same One Source, with your own center of awareness and perception in this physical dimension.

Your Expanded Self, who sees from the broad perspective of One Source, says an immediate *yes* to your genuine desires, and pulses powerfully with them. In any moment that you're vibrating with qualities such as peace, love, optimism, enthusiasm, appreciation, joy, satisfaction, delight, or blessedness, you are in the vibrational vicinity of your Expanded Self, and fresh thoughts of insight and inspiration can flow to you.

To summarize, *only active thoughts in your energy field or consciousness have creative power.* These are *thoughts you have accepted as true,* whether they align with what you want or not, and they generally fall into one or more of these categories:

The persuasive teachings, opinions, and conclusions of others.

Your own conclusions based on what you're observing, in your life and in the lives of others.

Thoughts vibrating powerfully in mass consciousness that may be resonant with active thoughts in your Local Self energy field.

Inspired thoughts that come to you from your own Expanded Self when you are in harmony with it.

The more firmly you accept them as true and the more familiar they have become to you, the stronger they are, which means they are more likely to generate physical manifestations.

Dominant beliefs on a subject create consistent results

Step back for a moment and consider the many active beliefs you have about various things. You've probably noticed that some of your beliefs contradict each other on any given topic. You may believe, for example, that this is an abundant Universe with plenty of money for everyone. Yet you may also believe that you're not worthy of experiencing abundance, or that you don't know how to access it, or perhaps that the greed, selfishness, or ignorance of others has kept it from you. If those contradictory beliefs are equivalent in strength, your experience of financial abundance is likely a two-steps-forward, two-steps-back kind of thing. Just when you think you're getting ahead, something happens and you're once again experiencing lack.

This is quite common. Our active beliefs on a subject can be equally strong in opposite directions, resulting in little movement toward what we want. What is also quite common is for us to have *dominant* beliefs on a subject—either dominantly in harmony with what we want or dominantly out of harmony with what we want.

The active, *dominant* vibrations in your personal energy field or consciousness regarding any area of your life determine the type of experiences you have in that area. Sometimes the relationship between what you believe and what you experience is direct and obvious. For example, if you were brought up in an environment of financial instability and that's what you continue to experience, you can easily recognize your dominant thoughts about money and where they came from.

In other areas of your life that may not be the case. Here is a different example of how things can manifest in your experience that don't seem directly related to your dominant beliefs.

Imagine that your life is humming along quite nicely. On your way to work one day, rain starts pouring down as an intense thunderstorm rolls through your area. Even though you're an excellent driver and have never had a bad experience in a thunderstorm, you freeze with panic as you drive. Your heart is pumping wildly and you're barely breathing. You talk yourself through the fear and arrive safely at work.

What happened?

Here's the backstory. For the past several days, as you've read various posts from neighbors on your favorite social media platform, you've learned about an increased number of robberies in your area. The tone of the messages is one of alarm, and everyone is urging caution. Although you didn't really pay attention at the time, you felt concern for your safety as you read the posts.

The vibration of vulnerability to threats, which is extremely active in the collective human consciousness, became strongly active in your personal consciousness. Without really considering it, this thought you had previously *accepted as true*—the thought that everyone, including you, is vulnerable to all kinds of unwanted things—gained sufficient strength to become momentarily dominant and generate a manifestation.

In the thunderstorm example, unlike the example of having grown up in a household in which money was tight, you didn't have direct, personal experiences of being harmed that generated a specific fear of thunderstorms. Yet a *general* fear of being harmed in some way had been more strongly activated in reading those posts. As you were driving in a particular situation that many people find scary, you were in harmonic resonance with that *specific* fear, which is vibrating powerfully in the collective consciousness.

In addition to illustrating how quickly a belief about a certain subject can become dominant, this example illustrates an important point about our personal experiences in relationship with the collective.

General beliefs in our personal consciousness, if they're strongly active and therefore dominant in any given moment, match us up with *specific* beliefs and memories in the collective consciousness that are in vibrational harmony with them, resulting in the specific experiences we have.

This dynamic between general beliefs and specific experiences is helpful to understand as part of our study of how specific beliefs are formed.

Beliefs are often formed from the general to the specific

We've been concluding things about ourselves and our lives since we were very young—things we accepted as true, which became beliefs. You've no doubt done a lot of deep, personal reflection and are aware of many things you came to believe that you now know do not serve you.

Yet you may also have experienced things in life that don't seem to line up with anything you specifically believe, such as the sudden panic in a thunderstorm in the previous example. Let's look at the primary dynamic giving rise to this: beliefs are often formed from the general to the specific, because general beliefs lead to specific experiences that are in vibrational harmony with them.

Let's say that throughout your childhood the belief that life isn't fair was something you heard countless times. It is strongly active in your Local Self consciousness. You're now a young adult working at your first full-time job, and one of your co-workers gets promoted to a position for which you think you are better qualified. The Law of Attraction has matched your general belief in the unfairness of life with a specific manifestation of it, from your perspective.

Feeling angry and betrayed, you conclude from this experience that your boss doesn't like you. This is a more specific conclusion—a more specific belief—than "life isn't fair." You hadn't believed it before you got passed over for promotion. It may have been a passing thought, but now it's a specific belief. The more specific the belief, the more focused it is. This new belief becomes the dominant vibration you have regarding your boss.

Shortly thereafter, your boss reprimands you in a meeting, which is an even more specific manifestation of your newly formed specific belief. After a few more instances like this, you conclude that your boss will never treat you fairly because he doesn't like you, and you've got to get a new job.

And so, you do. Yet you're still vibrating with "life isn't fair," and you've developed a little suspicion about bosses in general, having now heard— thanks to the Law of Attraction responding to your belief—many stories of people being unfairly treated by their supervisors. Not surprisingly, you start having similar experiences in your new job. At this point you conclude that, "It's not what you know, it's who you know." Or, if self-doubt has crept in, "I don't have what it takes to get ahead."

You can see in this example how experiences show up that don't match a specific belief you already hold, but vibrationally they match a more general one. And once the experience occurs, it not only reinforces your general belief, but it also gives rise to new, more specific ones.

This example also highlights that, as your belief about something intensifies—in this case, your belief that your boss doesn't like you, regardless of the good work you do—you start attracting more evidence of it, both in your own life as well as stories about it happening to others.

Bringing it all together

Only *active* beliefs in your Local Self energy field or consciousness can generate manifested results. Any thought you have *accepted as true* is an active belief. The more strongly you believe it, the stronger its vibration and the more likely it is to generate manifestations.

You likely have multiple active beliefs about any desire you have. When your beliefs are dominantly in harmony with what you want, what you want can manifest in your experience. When your beliefs are dominantly out of harmony with what you want, what you want cannot manifest.

Beliefs are usually formed from the general to the specific. General beliefs you hold, which are strongly active, will match up with more specific thoughts vibrating in mass consciousness, generating specific experiences. As you form conclusions about those specific experiences, you form new and more specific beliefs. These new beliefs can also generate matching manifested results if they are vibrating strongly enough.

Whose thought is it, anyway?

Let's revisit the understanding that creative power exists at the level of the individual. The examples offered in the previous sections may seem to indicate that creative power exists at the level of mass consciousness because they reveal how readily beliefs in mass consciousness can be accepted as beliefs in someone's personal, Local Self consciousness.

Yet the creative power to change beliefs resides with the *individual* because we have individual free will. While we are often influenced by others' vibrations in mass consciousness, *we don't have to be.*

Most of us don't know this, because most of us are not aware of the energetic properties of thought. We don't know how easily our dominant vibration can attract related yet different thoughts from mass consciousness that are in vibrational harmony with it. And we don't know about the power we have to consciously choose our thoughts.

Things can only manifest in our experience if we have accepted the underlying thoughts about them to be true and therefore possible *for us*. They don't manifest in our experience *because* the underlying thoughts about them are vibrating in mass consciousness. They manifest because our own personal consciousness is vibrating in a way that matches us up with them.

In effect, we say *yes* to things vibrating in mass consciousness by virtue of what's already vibrating in our Local Self consciousness. In the earlier example, your belief that life isn't fair is a *yes* to the thoughtform in mass consciousness vibrating with the belief that bosses do not treat their employees fairly.

This is not *yes* as in, "I agree with this," or "I want this." Rather, it is *yes* as in, "This is real or true and it could happen in my life."

We can learn to consciously back away from unwanted or limiting thoughts in mass consciousness and to cultivate thoughts that support our pure desires. We can exercise our free will to shift our personal consciousness through intention, awareness, willingness, and practice—what I refer to as the four portals of transformation—that we'll be learning more about in a later chapter. For the moment, I want to emphasize that we have the *innate ability* to make that shift.

What often makes it seem challenging or tricky is that we aren't fully aware of what we've accepted as true. We've got thoughts vibrating in our energy fields that have been repeated so often, by so many people, that they've become assumptions we simply take to be "what is." Many of them are thoughts that are strongly active in mass consciousness. They came in through the back door of a more general belief we already held, without our express knowledge or invitation.

In other words, we've got thoughts vibrating in our energy fields that we didn't mindfully evaluate before saying *yes* to them.

Is this why we need to reprogram the subconscious mind?

You've no doubt heard the term "subconscious" to describe thoughts of which you are unaware, but that actively generate manifestations, often unwanted ones. If so, you may have been taught that you need to "reprogram" your subconscious mind, as one might reprogram a computer, to generate desired results.

My personal preference is to move away from any perspective that views humans like computers or machines. While such analogies can initially be useful in helping people migrate from their current understanding to a new one, over time they artificially limit our Self-perception. We are vastly more than any machine or computer ever created. We are magnificent, powerful, and infinitely creative beings who have barely tapped into our brilliance and our unlimited potentials.

So, how do we deal with unrecognized thoughts that are generating unwanted manifestations? Rather than thinking of them as subconscious thoughts that are outside of our conscious control, I prefer to think of them simply as *active thoughts we aren't aware we are holding.*

The good news is that many, perhaps most, of these thoughts are much closer to our awareness than we think. As we learn to quiet our minds and reflect, they often reveal themselves to us easily.

And perhaps more importantly, we don't actually need to know which thoughts, specifically, are creating unwanted manifestations. Often, they are general, firmly entrenched thoughts vibrating powerfully in mass consciousness that we've accepted as true, such as beliefs in our vulnerability.

Whether the unrecognized thoughts are general or specific, if they are creating unwanted manifestations, the most wise and loving response we can offer is this:

We can use the experience to help us clarify what we *do* want, and then choose to focus on thought patterns that support our newly honed desire. As we focus on these supportive thoughts *now* and *now* and *now*, they become stronger and more stable, until they become dominant.

Remember, thoughts become active because we are focusing on them in the present moment, or because we've already accepted them as true. We can render inactive the unhelpful thoughts we previously accepted as true—whether we're specifically aware of them or not—by calling on our present power of focus to help us accept new, supportive thoughts as true.

Creating a consciousness of self-love

This is a significant dynamic to understand and embrace. Over the years, many people have been digging for the limiting or painful beliefs that have prevented what they want from flowing into their physical experience. They try all kinds of things to eliminate those beliefs, including various methods to reprogram their subconscious, only to realize after years of working on their "issues" that they're not significantly more fulfilled than when they started.

Digging for false and painful beliefs is both unnecessary and impractical for several reasons. First, what we focus on is what we activate and strengthen in our Now moment. Often, as we focus on an unwanted manifestation and what may have given rise to it, we activate a lot of thoughts about the unwanted experience as we try to figure things out. In those moments, we're focusing on what we don't want and are therefore strengthening the very thoughtforms that may give rise to *more* of what we don't want. And we're attracting into our awareness more memories, examples, and thoughts that match what we're digging for, rendering the search virtually endless.

In addition, digging for false and painful beliefs often activates the profoundly untrue and unhelpful belief that there is something wrong with us, some flaw we must overcome. Strengthening that painful belief can only lead to unsatisfying experiences.

Another factor to consider is that not every false belief we hold is problematic for us, personally. For example, you might falsely believe that artists have a difficult time making good money. But if you're an engineer with a satisfying corporate career, that belief probably isn't getting in your way.

For these reasons, I do not encourage people to dig deeply for false, unhelpful thought patterns that may be generating unwanted manifestations. We can use our understanding of active, dominant beliefs and how they are formed from the general to the specific, as well as our understanding of the power of our present focus, to cultivate new, supportive beliefs into dominance in our energy fields.

I want to offer a key distinction: while *digging* for false beliefs and where they came from is neither helpful nor practical, these two activities are extremely helpful:

> *Reflecting* on the dynamic of how your dominant thoughts about things have manifested in your physical experience.

> *Paying attention*, in your present life experience, to the relationship between how you think and feel and the kinds of things showing up in your life.

With a loving intention for expanded self-awareness, reflection helps you understand that the dynamic between thought and manifestation is real. Without understanding that, you have little reason to practice changing the way you think. It wasn't until I reread those self-diminishing journal entries that I realized how powerful my thoughts really are.

The key to effective reflection in this area is to *scan* rather than dig. Step back and reflect on major events of your life and see if you can recognize the patterns of thought you may have been holding at those times which generated the experiences you had.

Paying attention to how you're thinking and feeling *now*, and how that relates to what you're experiencing *now*, reinforces your understanding of the dynamic and further helps you recognize the power of every present moment. You don't need to go back into your past to "undo" things. If a belief formed in your past is generating unwanted manifestations now, that means it is active now and can be rendered inactive now.

The distinction between digging and reflecting is a subtle but essential one which requires a clear intention to maintain. Sometimes what starts out as a curious inquiry into how you manifested something can morph into a search-and-destroy mission, aimed at the false and painful beliefs you desperately want to uncover.

The key to maintaining a loving intention for expanded self-awareness, rather than slipping into old habits of finding fault with yourself, lies in staying close to how you feel. If you start feeling discouraged, despairing, guilty, resentful, or any other uncomfortable emotion, *stop*. The uncomfortable feeling is your signal that you've veered away from the clear, helpful, and loving perspective of your Expanded Self. Take a few deep breaths and shift your attention to something that feels better.

I want to emphasize here that my intention in explaining in some depth the various nuances of how thoughts lead to manifested experiences is to help you *better understand the dynamic.* While manifestations may seem random, there is always a vibrational basis for them that follows the consistent Law of Attraction and its response to our active, dominant beliefs. We gain greater mastery over what we manifest as we gain greater awareness of how we're vibrating.

However, once the basic dynamic is understood, we don't benefit by laboriously analyzing everything that manifests in our lives. Our opportunity is to use what we've learned to reinforce our commitment to loving ourselves forward, rather than pushing and criticizing ourselves forward. Knowing how powerful our thoughts really are, we see that loving ourselves forward is the only sane approach to take.

Reflection Point

I have free will. Therefore, I have the ability to cultivate beliefs that are in harmony with my desires, regardless of what others believe and experience. I am sovereign in my world.

8

THE POWER & PURPOSE
OF EMOTION

As thought goes, emotion flows.

Years ago, during one of the wobbly times in my transition from corporate employee to writer and teacher, I was feeling anxious about my finances and uncertain about whether I should stay in the home I loved or sell it. On one particularly anxiety-ridden day, a friend called, and I shared my concerns and frustrations with her. As I listened in stunned disbelief, she brought up additional issues of concern that I hadn't even considered. My anxiety mushroomed into full-blown fear, and along with it came anger at her for being so insensitive.

I couldn't get off the phone fast enough. My uncomfortable emotions were almost overwhelming me, and I didn't want to say anything I would later regret. I found some reason to end the call, then immediately went into my living room and got down on the floor, in child's pose. I intentionally slowed and deepened my breathing as I reminded myself of certain truths:

"This is not about her, it's about me. This is *for* me."

"Life is always on my side."

"There is only one true power in this universe, and it is Love."

I repeated them silently to myself, over and over, as I continued breathing through my feelings with my forehead pressed to the floor. After several minutes, I felt a shift. My body relaxed as the stormy emotions retreated, and in the space where they had been I found a precious and welcome sense of peace. Sweet, sweet peace. I stayed where I was, breathing deeply and relishing how I felt.

A few minutes later, the phone rang. I got up and walked calmly into the kitchen to answer it. It was my friend, calling back. She said, in a kind and quiet voice, "Suzanne, I'm sorry. I don't think I'm supporting you in the way you need to be supported." And we proceeded to have a kind and respectful conversation.

That experience revealed a lot to me about the dance of thought and emotion, the way the Law of Attraction always brings to us that which matches our dominant vibration, and the power we have in the present moment to shift from the unwanted to the wanted.

Thought and emotion: two aspects of the same dynamic

Human emotions are one of the most misunderstood aspects of our life experience. Alternately vilified as the root of hurtful behavior and celebrated as the impetus for creative self-expression, our emotions are often experienced as something capricious and outside our conscious control. This can leave us feeling vulnerable to them and therefore wary of them.

I've been curious about the role emotions play in our lives for decades, stimulated initially by my fascination with Mr. Spock, a lead character in the original *Star Trek* series to whom I was introduced years later, when the *Star Trek* movies were released. Because of his Vulcan upbringing, he had learned to suppress his emotions. Vulcans, you see, prize logic above all else and deem emotions to be detrimental to mental clarity. I found the fictional character of Mr. Spock both likeable and admirable. He could be counted on to assess challenging situations quickly and accurately, and to come up with well-considered solutions that he would always present in a respectful manner. Who wouldn't want Mr. Spock on their team?

As I progressed in my corporate career, I found myself leaning more in Mr. Spock's direction. I observed that business decisions—ones I didn't think were sound—were often made from a personally emotional place, not from a logical one that considered the needs of the whole. I also couldn't help but notice that my own actions, when initiated from an emotionally reactive place, never yielded favorable results. My questions about the value of emotions intensified.

It was through my training as an energy healer at the Barbara Brennan School of Healing, followed by my introduction to the teachings of Abraham, that I came to understand the power and purpose of human emotions, which are neither capricious nor outside the influence and direction of our conscious mind.

At the Brennan school, I learned that emotional energy associated with painful thoughts can block the radiance of our Expanded Self from being seen, felt, and experienced. I also learned that emotion always follows thought. Later, Abraham's simple and direct description of emotions as *guidance* put my then-current understanding of emotional energy into an even clearer and more helpful perspective.

As with everything else in this vibrational universe, emotions are a form of energy, and they have a particular purpose. Our emotions indicate the degree to which our Local Self thoughts are in harmony with the perspective of our Expanded Self. The better we feel, the more in harmony we are with our Expanded Self. The worse we feel, the less in harmony we are with our Expanded Self.

The frequencies of our emotions relate directly to the frequencies of our Local Self thoughts. Thought energy is electrical in nature, and emotional energy is its magnetic counterpart. Thought/emotion is an inseparable, electromagnetic dynamic, to which the Law of Attraction is responding. To be very clear, emotions exist only in partnership with our thoughts.

This may not seem to be the case in moments of near-instantaneous emotional reactions to things or situations. However, just because an emotional reaction happens quickly doesn't mean it's without thought—or, more precisely, without *meaning*. Remember, a thought doesn't have to be expressed through language. The essence of thought is the perspective it represents.

For example, the perspective that the emotion of anger often represents is, "This is wrong, and it shouldn't be happening!" That specific phrase may or may not come to mind when anger is activated quickly in someone, but its meaning—the way that person interprets what is happening—is what determines the emotion she feels as anger. In a very real way, our emotions are the *felt sense* of our wordless thoughts.

Emotions as guidance

As noted above, the better we feel emotionally, the more in harmony our Local Self thoughts are with our Expanded Self perspective. The worse we feel emotionally, the less in harmony our Local Self thoughts are with our Expanded Self perspective. Since our Expanded Self says an immediate *yes* to our Local Self desires and therefore vibrates with them, this means that the better we feel emotionally, the more in harmony we are with our genuine desires, and the worse we feel emotionally, the less in harmony we are with our genuine desires.

It's important to understand that the thoughts giving rise to uncomfortable emotions—and therefore indicating that we're not in harmony with our desires—do not always have to be directly related to our known desires. For example, let's assume you have a desire for greater financial abundance in your life. Your current thought patterns about money are not in alignment with prosperity, so you begin to consciously cultivate thoughts that specifically reflect an abundance mindset.

Consider now the feeling state of financial abundance. It's a good-feeling place—perhaps for you it feels like freedom and generosity. You can cultivate thoughts about money that move you in that direction, but if you frequently hold thoughts about other areas of your life that generate emotions such as frustration, worry or resentment, those vibrational frequencies—which are not in harmony with the frequencies of abundance—can slow down or stall your manifestation of the abundance you desire.

In other words, the better you feel in general, the more likely you are to manifest *any* of your specific desires, and the worse you feel in general, the less likely you are to manifest any of your specific desires.

You can, however, feel very good in general about your life, yet still not manifest a desire that's important to you because your specific thoughts about that subject are strongly in opposition to it. Conversely, you can feel not-so-good-about your life in general, but if your desire for something specific is very strong, and your thoughts about that desire are mostly in alignment with it, it can manifest.

The key point here is that whenever we feel uncomfortable emotions, we render *unhelpful* thoughts active. The uncomfortable emotion is our signal to shift our focus toward thoughts that feel better. This is the essence of how emotions guide us: we acknowledge that we are feeling emotionally uncomfortable, then redirect our attention to better-feeling thoughts.

It is a simple and elegant design, yet it can be challenging in practice, depending on how strongly and how quickly the uncomfortable emotion surfaces, and depending also on how well acquainted we are with loving, helpful thoughts.

Are we shifting or pasting over?

After years of exposure to the ideas of positive thinking and positive affirmations, many people try immediately to think of something positive when they experience an uncomfortable emotion. This is rarely effective, and it often results in feeling like we're lying to ourselves, which lowers our vibration even further. I refer to this effort as a paste-over. Rather than genuinely moving our thoughts in a helpful direction, we make a positive statement *while still feeling uncomfortable.*

The uncomfortable feeling is our indicator that the unhelpful thoughts are still active and dominant, even if we haven't translated them into words. And the Law of Attraction is responding to our active and dominant vibration—as indicated by the way we feel—regardless of the specific words we may be thinking or speaking in any moment.

The good news is, making a genuine shift in vibration, rather than simply pasting over an uncomfortable feeling, can be easily learned, practiced, and mastered. It's a matter of intentionality and discernment. Here are the essential steps:

Acknowledge—admit to yourself that you're experiencing an uncomfortable feeling.

Pause—take a deep breath (or several).

Intend—commit internally to the importance of feeling better *now.*

Redirect—shift your focus to something else.

Feel for improvement—notice if you're feeling emotionally better or, at least, neutral.

We will review this practice in depth in a later chapter, although with this introduction, you can experiment and begin making genuine improvements in your vibrational stance right now.

The first step is often a very beneficial practice of its own. *Pay attention to how you feel* as you move through your day, regardless of whether the feelings are comfortable or uncomfortable. Perhaps the best way to practice this is to pause at the conclusion of each activity and check in with yourself to see how you feel. Doing this helps you become more aware of the range of feelings you have, as well as your general emotional set point.

Many of us have been conditioned to ignore or suppress how we really feel, so we've lost touch with our emotions. Additionally, we've become so accustomed to feelings such as anxiety, worry, frustration, and impatience, that we consider them normal. We don't see them as indicators of a needed change in focus.

So, intend to "turn up the dial of self-awareness," as I often say, from here moving forward. Reacquaint yourself with your true feelings, without judgment or analysis. Just notice, and when you can do so in moments of feeling uncomfortable, experiment with the practice of acknowledging, pausing to take some deep breaths, intending to feel better, shifting focus and sensing again how you feel.

I want to point out that I'm intentionally using words such as "uncomfortable" and "comfortable" to describe categories of emotions, rather than "negative" and "positive." Given their essential purpose in guiding us toward thought patterns that harmonize with our desires, all emotions are helpful and, in that regard, positive. Labeling uncomfortable feelings as negative can engender judgmental thoughts about ourselves for having those feelings. And we know that self-judgment will never bring us closer to our desires.

Similarly, thinking about "positive" emotions with regard to redirecting our thoughts can encourage the use of the paste-over. Rather than trying to be positive when we're not feeling that way, my encouragement is to find thoughts that are loving, soothing, or supportive. These kinds of thoughts can help us to genuinely feel our way to a better-feeling place. We'll explore various examples of this in part three.

When emotions seem to be getting the better of us

Sometimes our uncomfortable emotions are so strong, or arise so quickly, that the process described above isn't possible to execute. At those times we can do something else that is simple, subtle, and highly effective: we can mindfully and intentionally *feel* our feelings.

The key to this practice is to set aside any thought we're holding that justifies how we're feeling as we lovingly direct our attention into our *bodies*, wherever the emotion can be most strongly felt. We notice and sense all the emotion's nuances, intending to experience the emotion as what it is: *energy*, vibrating in a particular way in that moment. No judgments, no justifications, no analysis. Just breathing and feeling, breathing and feeling, breathing and feeling, until the wave of emotion subsides, and we come to a place of neutrality or experience any emotion that simply feels better.

The most challenging aspect of this practice is the initial shift in focus *away* from whatever triggered the emotion, toward our own *inner* experience. In my reaction to what my friend said in our telephone conversation, I used the anchor statements I shared with you to help me do that. I focused on those self-generated thoughts so I could release my focus on all the blaming thoughts that were racing through my mind about her.

This practice doesn't *require* such statements, however. It simply requires a clear and firm intention to shift focus from the *object* of our emotional reaction to the *reaction, itself.* When we do that with an open heart, we create a safe inner environment in which the cycle of that emotional pulse can be completed. Once the emotion has subsided, we can then redirect our focus in a loving, supportive way toward something else.

In general, the practice of simply feeling our feelings works better when the feeling is very strong, and the practice of pausing to redirect our thoughts works better when the feeling is relatively slight. The essential elements of both approaches are nonresistance, an open heart, and a conscious intention to respond to uncomfortable emotion in a healthy way.

These practices are, essentially, acts of Self Love. They are ways to reinforce within ourselves the understanding that we matter, and how we feel matters. They are ways of being kind to ourselves rather than being critical. They are responsible ways to deal with our emotions and they fortify our self-respect.

So, what are our emotions telling us?

Knowing how to navigate through uncomfortable emotions, lovingly and responsibly, is essential on the path of awakening to more and more of who we are. Equally important is an understanding of how Local Self thoughts that give rise to uncomfortable emotions differ from the perspective of our Expanded Self. In the absence of that understanding, we are likely to maintain unhelpful patterns of thought.

Let's consider a common family of Local Self thought that generates uncomfortable feelings: judgmental and doubting thoughts about ourselves—thoughts that diminish, demean, or limit us in some way. Our Expanded Self knows us as beloved and gloriously unique extensions of One Source, imbued with the love, wisdom, and power to realize our desires and live deeply fulfilling lives. When we think of ourselves as less than that, we experience uncomfortable emotions.

I have found that a simple way to shift my focus away from habitual thoughts of self-doubt or self-criticism is to ask myself a question such as:

"What is the most self-loving thing I could think or do right now?"

"What is a kinder and more respectful way to look at this?"

"How does my Expanded Self view this moment?"

Over time, as I have become clearer about the *profound* unhelpfulness of critical thoughts about myself, and therefore more committed to rendering them inactive, I have learned to say a loving but very firm *no* to those thoughts, often with the phrase, "This thought has nothing to do with who I am."

We will continue to explore ways to cultivate a consciousness of genuine Self-Love as we move through the remaining chapters. Let's turn now to another family of thought that is often more difficult to recognize as needing to be shifted, even though it gives rise to very uncomfortable emotions: thoughts of judgment, blame, condemnation, or fear of others.

Remember that our uncomfortable emotions are a signal that whatever we're thinking in that moment is not in alignment with the perspective of our Expanded Self, which means it is not in harmony with our desires. So when, for example, we see someone else as an obstacle to our happiness, the cause of our pain, or the reason why so many bad things are happening, our uncomfortable emotions of anger, frustration, or resentment are telling us that our Expanded Self is not seeing them the same way.

Our Expanded Self sees every person on this planet as a beloved and gloriously unique extension of One Source, in varying degrees of self-awareness of that truth. People who are acting in harmful ways to themselves and others have almost no awareness of that truth; they are living in separation consciousness, which is the only level of consciousness from which harmful thoughts and actions can arise. But that does not change who they fundamentally are as extensions of One Source.

Aside from those who are acting out in clearly destructive and hurtful ways, there are many people on the planet and in our lives whose Local Self perspective is very different than our own. We don't often agree on values and priorities. And when one of those people is, say, our life partner, it can certainly seem that his or her refusal to agree with us is the reason why we're not experiencing what we want. Or when a rude cashier closes the checkout lane just as we're stepping into line, it can seem as if the cashier is the problem.

And yet, that's not how our Expanded Self sees them. If it was, we wouldn't be feeling uncomfortable emotions. It isn't that our Expanded Self can't recognize rude or otherwise destructive behaviors, or that it condones such behaviors. It's that our Expanded Self knows how powerful and worthy we are, how infinitely creative and abundant this universe is, and how the essence of all our desires can be met regardless of what anyone else is doing.

As long as we aren't stubbornly focused on what they're doing that we don't like.

In other words, our Expanded Self never thinks the kind of thoughts we think as we observe something unwanted or disliked. We see them as the reasons why we aren't happy, content, successful, or healthy. We effectively *give our power away* to those unwanted conditions. Our Expanded Self knows the only reason we're not happy is because we're not in vibrational harmony with happiness, and that we have the power to come into vibrational harmony with it.

We benefit ourselves greatly by understanding that continuing to focus on people or situations that upset us holds us apart from desires that could otherwise manifest—including desired solutions to the problems we're observing—and by consistently shifting our focus toward what we want.

Many people call this "putting our heads in the sand," which is another version of what I call the paste-over. But we're not pasting over anything, or ignoring anything important, when we have *acknowledged* it as unwanted and then have intentionally chosen to move toward what is wanted.

This is a subtle but vital distinction to grasp. If we feel an uncomfortable emotion and try to ignore it because it's painful, we haven't accomplished anything. It's still vibrating, and we're still attracting thoughts and experiences on that same frequency. But if we feel an uncomfortable emotion and recognize that our thoughts of powerlessness are the cause of it, and then take responsibility for shifting our thoughts, we are constructively moving forward. As Einstein wisely said, "No problem can be solved from the same level of consciousness that created it."

Finding a new perspective

We can begin cultivating perspectives that are in alignment with our Expanded Self by reflecting on the foundational concepts offered in part one and imagining what our Expanded Self perspective might be in any given situation.

Here are examples of thoughts that are helpful to cultivate. They are based on the understanding that we are individual extensions of One Source, and we are vibrational beings with free will. We can think of them as thoughts our Expanded Self holds about us and about life. I've chosen to write them in the second person, as if your Expanded Self is talking directly to you:

> You are dearly loved, and you are meant to thrive and enjoy life.

> You have the ability to shift your focus, and therefore your vibration, to attract different experiences.

> It's not your job to change or "fix" anyone else. Nothing is broken. Everyone is living, learning, and growing at their own pace, in accordance with their free will choices.

> Your creative power arises through your harmony with One Source. It is not dependent on what anyone thinks, says or does.

In the story I shared with you about the painful conversation with my friend, I benefited greatly by remembering these things, and by taking them a step further. I reminded myself that she wouldn't have said the unhelpful things she said, or I wouldn't have interpreted them as painful, had I not already been vibrating with similar thoughts and feelings. In other words, because of the Law of Attraction, I effectively evoked those statements from her through the vibration of my own dominant, unhelpful thoughts.

In remembering that, I took back the power I had attributed to her. Then I intentionally focused on helpful, soothing, and ultimately empowering thoughts, and our next interaction reflected that.

Don't we have to process painful feelings?

The question of whether we benefit from processing painful feelings is a different way of asking whether we need to look for the origin of our painful beliefs. Let's consider this with our clarified understanding of the power and purpose of emotions.

My answer to the question of whether we must "process" painful feelings by looking into our past for the origin of the painful beliefs giving rise to them is no. It isn't a requirement for moving forward into a life of ever-deepening fulfillment.

What I have come to realize is that the origin of *all* painful beliefs is the false premise of our separation from One Source. And having realized that, I further understand that the only way to render that profoundly false belief inactive is by consciously activating new thoughts of empowerment, stemming from an understanding of who we really are.

I recognize, however, that my pivotal realization about the origin of all painful beliefs came to me after having discovered the seeming "original cause" of various painful beliefs I've held in this lifetime. In other words, in doing some "processing," I was able to see that all the painful beliefs I uncovered came from the same root.

And I often had a sense of satisfaction in "connecting the dots," in recognizing patterns of thought that developed from conclusions I'd drawn from early, painful experiences and, most importantly, in recognizing that those conclusions had nothing to do with where I was at the time. Sometimes just understanding that was all I needed to let the belief go.

Most times, however, simply recognizing the painful belief and how it originated in my life wasn't sufficient to render it inactive. It still had a lot of strength and stability in my consciousness. I still had to learn how to activate new, loving, and empowering thoughts. And often, the process of digging for the belief and its origins was frustrating or even depressing as I recalled painful memories. Those feelings were indicators that I was not in harmony with my Expanded Self.

So, my strong encouragement is to place primary emphasis on the cultivation of loving and empowering thoughts about yourself and your life, letting your current uncomfortable emotions show you where you need to reinforce them. Choose to spend very little time going back into your past to uncover painful beliefs you may have formed at an earlier age. If they are beneficial for you to know, they will surface in your awareness when you are in vibrational harmony with your Expanded Self.

My friend's comments reflected my fear of being stupid—in this case, stupid for not having thought of them myself. Did it matter that my fear of being stupid might have come from early childhood experiences in which I witnessed my brother being physically and harshly punished for being "stupid"? No.

What mattered is that I recognized how I felt in the moment of the conversation, and that helped me recognize how I wanted to feel: safe, competent, and loved. I knew the direction in which I needed to focus my attention and my thoughts.

What is tremendously helpful and important to remember from the previous chapter is that even active thoughts that are *outside* of our normal sphere of awareness, which can generate unwanted manifestations and uncomfortable emotional reactions to them, can be rendered inactive by consciously focusing *now* and *now* and *now* on thoughts we want to strengthen and stabilize. Through our loving persistence the new, supportive thoughts become dominant, and once that occurs, it doesn't matter whether the painful belief we formerly held was actively vibrating in our sphere of awareness, or outside of it.

If you still feel strongly drawn to uncovering "old" painful beliefs beneath your current painful emotions, please tread lightly. Scan, but don't dig. Be sure your intention is for expanded self-awareness and liberation from limiting beliefs, not fault-finding. Pay attention to how you feel as you search. Do not let yourself stay long in feelings of fear, frustration, confusion, impatience, sadness, depression, or any other uncomfortable emotion. Suspend your search and move on. Trust that whatever insights you need will come to you when you're feeling relaxed.

Reflection Point

How I feel indicates whether my thoughts are in alignment with the perspective of my Expanded Self. As I pay attention to my feelings and commit to feeling as good as I can, I come into vibrational harmony with my desires.

9

THE GIFT OF
INNER GUIDANCE

Your Expanded Self vibrates not only with the purity of your desires, but also with the wisdom to guide you to their realization.

I had gone back to the corporate world for what would be my last time. I could feel the desire to do work I truly loved was becoming stronger. I knew I would one day leave my corporate career and not look back. I just didn't know when.

Yet I trusted that when the time came, I *would* know. I had learned to recognize the ways my inner guidance reveals itself to me, and I had practiced following it. I was ready for the signal, not knowing exactly what form it would take.

One day, during a pause in my at-home, make-it-up-as-I-go-along dance routine (which was my favorite form of cardio workout), I stood by the large sliding glass door in my living room. My mind was quiet as I caught my breath, gazing at the trees across the street and the city skyline in the distance. Although the sun was shining, it seemed as if the office buildings were shrouded in mist. As I watched, the mist began to clear. And then, in the stillness of my mind, a single thought arose: *Now is the time.*

I knew without a shadow of a doubt that it was specific guidance to leave my corporate job. I felt deeply at peace. Within days, I had resigned. And I've never looked back.

I have, of course, had many wobbly moments of not knowing how to move forward. That's why I decided I had to learn to love myself forward, step by step, rather than continuing to allow doubt and fear to stop me. A significant aspect of that learning was how to recognize, trust and follow my own inner wisdom.

The most fundamental expression of inner guidance anyone has is desire itself. Desire is the very essence of guidance, calling us forward in a particular direction. We *exist because of desire, and just as desire establishes our beingness, it guides our ongoing evolution into more.* So, the exploration, recognition, and embrace of our genuine desires is a central element of cultivating inner guidance.

Additionally, our emotions reveal to us how closely aligned we are, in any moment, with our desires. Desire calls us in a particular direction. When we pay attention to how we feel, and we adjust our focus and thoughts to bring us back into harmony with those desires when we have strayed off course, we keep moving in that direction.

Desire and emotions are the only guidance we truly require on this journey of awakening to more and more of who we really are. Yet as we continue to honor our genuine desires, and start paying closer attention to how we feel, something wonderful happens: we develop a keener awareness of our inner state of being, and the ability to discern thoughts and impulses that come from our Expanded Self rather than our everyday thought patterns. This is what I experienced that pivotal morning in my living room and have experienced many times since then.

How do you know that you know?

As a student of healing science at the Barbara Brennan School of Healing, I benefited enormously from teachings that were specifically focused on helping us develop what was called High Sense Perception, or the ability to sense helpful and relevant information beyond what our physical senses can detect. The emphasis on learning to receive, recognize, and trust information from a deeper place of knowing was immensely valuable.

As we practiced identifying different streams of information (in the form of thought, images, sounds, kinesthetic sensing, or a somatic response), and drawing conclusions about whether they were valid and helpful, the teachers asked us repeatedly, "How do you know that you know?" Confused by the question at first, I soon figured out that they were asking us to identify the basis on which we knew that what we were receiving, or sensing, was coming from a reliable source. They were helping us develop keener levels of inner discernment.

The reliable source of valid and helpful information about next steps on our journey of awakening is, of course, One Source, as communicated to us through our Expanded Self. And part of the fun and mystery of the journey is learning to decipher its messages. Even those that come through in simple language, such as the message I received about that moment being the time to leave my corporate job, must be recognized as coming from the Expanded Self before accepting them and acting on them.

So, the question we benefit from asking ourselves is, "How do I know this _____ (idea, suggestion, information, image, sensation) is coming from my Expanded Self?" Although the specific answers to this question are unique to each person, you can find your answers more easily as you pay attention to the following:

Your emotional state of being at the time of receiving or sensing the guidance

As we explored in the previous chapter, the better you feel emotionally, the more in harmony you are with your desires and your Expanded Self. The same words, coming from different emotional states of being, can be vastly different in their helpfulness. For example, had I been frustrated or impatient, rather than calm and clear-minded, when the thought, "Now is the time" came to me, it likely would not have been from my Expanded Self. It would simply have been a thought I attracted that matched the vibrational frequency I was on.

The way the guidance itself feels as it shows up

This is difficult to articulate, and it may not be relevant to everyone, but I have noticed that loving and helpful guidance from my Expanded Self has a certain *feel* to it. The best way for me to describe the feeling I get is that it's peaceful and spacious. There is no rush, no urgency, no alarm. Referring again to the example of my experience, had I heard, "Now is the time," when I was feeling frustrated with my job, it likely would have felt very defiant or impatient.

The nature of the guidance itself

Helpful guidance is usually brief and to the point, and it's always loving and supportive. Your Expanded Self would never guide you to say or do something harmful, or speak to you in a harsh, belittling, or demeaning way. Also, your Expanded Self would never guide you to do something you are currently afraid to do. However, if you have strong doubt or anxiety about something you desire, your Expanded Self will encourage you in the *direction* of your desire. But it will not direct you to take any action that frightens you.

How you feel about the guidance

Wise and loving guidance from the Expanded Self feels that way. It often feels comforting or inspiring, but sometimes you simply get a sense that it is "right" or true for you, like something you've known but haven't yet admitted to yourself. You might feel a relieved sense of, "Yes, that's it," or something similar to that kind of feeling.

There is clearly a lot of overlap in these categories, but I offer them separately because there are subtle distinctions among them, and one description might resonate with you more strongly than others. These same guidelines hold true whether the guidance you receive is in words, images, symbols, feelings, dreams, or some other form.

An additional criterion to help you assess whether guidance is coming from your Expanded Self is that its meaning is both clear and helpful to you. This is of particular relevance when the guidance doesn't come through in words. However, clarity and meaning may require a little sleuthing to uncover, particularly when you're interpreting a dream! That's part of what makes this intriguing and satisfying.

If a dream or image is difficult to interpret, or if your interpretation doesn't feel good, helpful, or "right" to you, chances are it didn't come from your Expanded Self—or you're interpreting it when you are not in harmony with your Expanded Self. Set it aside, focus on maintaining a stable emotional state that feels good, and know that guidance will continue to be offered to you.

Common forms of guidance and how to be ready for them

There are probably as many unique forms of guidance as there are people, yet in my work with clients over the years these forms of guidance have surfaced frequently and helpfully:

Direct knowing

You suddenly know or realize something, often in a moment when your mind is elsewhere, without having researched or analyzed it. It's what happened in my, "Now is the time," moment. It often arrives in direct words, but it can also come through as a feeling or image that you can immediately translate into something meaningful.

Felt sense of yes *or* no

As you consider a particular opportunity, you recognize bodily sensations that indicate whether it is beneficial for you. One caveat here is to be very clear about your emotional state before the sensation arises. If you're in an anxious or frustrated state, for example, your *yes* or *no* likely arises from your anxious or frustrated thoughts and not from your Expanded Self. It's always beneficial to cultivate as peaceful a state of mind before making decisions of any kind.

In-the-moment impulses

These are unexpected ideas that come to you outside of your normal habits of thought or behavior. They are usually simple and easy to follow through on, such as taking a different route to work, or signing up for a course you'd heard about a week ago but haven't thought of since then. Following them leads to something delightful or helpful or satisfying. Again, the key to trusting these impulses is being aware of your emotional state of being when they arise. If you're feeling good—clear, peaceful, optimistic, expansive, calm—they're likely coming from your Expanded Self.

Preferences

These are softer, gentler expressions of desire. They, like the seemingly larger desires for things such as satisfying work, are worthy of your *yes*. Honoring your genuine preferences as often as you can reinforces within your consciousness that you matter, and what you love matters. Strengthening this sense of worthiness puts you in vibrational range of all your desires, including the seemingly big ones.

The practices offered in later chapters will help you develop your ability to receive these, and other, forms of guidance. Fundamentally, though, it is through cultivation of a calm, clear mind—with a correspondingly calm and clear emotional state of being—that we become open to sound guidance from our Expanded Self. Any practice or activity you love that quiets your mind and lifts your spirits can open you to receive messages from your Expanded Self.

Signs, symbols, and synchronicities

The forms of guidance we've reviewed to this point are those that arise from within us. Others show up in our external world as signs, symbols, and synchronicities. Our experience of them is usually one of appreciation, delight, or even joy. They greatly enhance the fun factor on our journey of awakening.

I will never forget one such experience I had several years ago. I had been invited to submit a proposal for a TEDx Wilmington talk and I knew almost immediately what my talk would be about. Yet I grappled with what its title should be. I wanted it to be something that would be intriguing enough for people to want to listen.

One idea that came to me, *The Dark Side of Self Improvement*, was starkly different from the titles I typically use for my articles, talks and courses. Normally, I choose titles that focus on what is wanted, not what is unwanted. The central message of my talk was about learning to trust one's inner wisdom, and to initiate personal change from a place of self-loving desire, not from the flawed premise that there is something wrong that needs to be fixed. I kept playing with titles such as *Loving Yourself Forward*, but the "dark side" title idea wouldn't leave me alone.

Still, I couldn't quite bring myself to choose it.

One day, as I was bustling about town, running errands and feeling very productive, I found myself waiting in line at the shipping store. I took a few minutes to focus inward and ask my Expanded Self to give me the name of my TEDx talk. Then I was called to the counter and my focus returned to the matter at hand.

When I got in my car after leaving the store, I turned on the radio. I could barely believe what I was hearing: *On the Dark Side*, by Eddie and the

Cruisers. I had no doubt that that was the answer to my request, and I laughed out loud, alone in my car. Later, I submitted my idea for a TEDx talk called *The Dark Side of Self Improvement* and it was accepted quickly. To this day, the TEDx talk stands out as one of the most satisfying and generative experiences I've had in my career.

The types of signs, symbols and synchronicities that can show up are limitless. Some of them are very specific—like hearing a song with "dark side" in the title—while others are more general in nature, such as seeing 11:11 on a digital clock and feeling that it's special. I usually interpret signs in the latter category as affirming that I'm on the right track. I'm in the flow of my beautiful life.

We know it is our Expanded Self who orchestrates these delightful experiences by the way we feel and by their helpfulness in answering a question we're contemplating, pointing us in a particular direction, or bringing us comfort, validation, or inspiration. As with guidance that comes to us in other forms, we receive these external confirmations when we are in an emotionally clear, good-feeling, and stable place.

Don't give your power away to "the universe"

There is something very important to understand about external signs or synchronicities that I learned years ago, a gift that arrived in another wobbly moment regarding my house. At that time, I was strongly considering leasing it to someone for a while, rather than selling it, and living in a less expensive place. I didn't love the idea, but I disliked it less than selling the house outright.

I happened to mention my idea to a friend in a brief conversation. The next day, she called to tell me that a friend and colleague of hers from Europe was coming to the United States for an extended assignment and wanted to lease a home in Wilmington, near the downtown area. Knowing him as well as she did, she thought my house would be perfect for him and his wife; and knowing *me* as well as she did, she thought that they would be ideal tenants for me. She had mentioned our conversation to him, and he was very interested in seeing my house.

I was stunned. What are the chances that such a perfect solution could materialize so quickly? It appeared to be a sign from the Universe that this was my path forward.

There was only one problem with it. I didn't want to do it. As perfect as my house might have been for them, the thought that kept repeating itself in my mind was that my house was perfect for *me*. I wanted to stay in it.

The swift and synchronous manifestation of my leasing idea wasn't a sign from the Universe that I should do it. It was a *manifestation of my dominant vibration*. Having focused with such intensity on options I didn't want, one of them manifested. And when it did, my reaction to it immediately clarified for me what I *did* want. I was thankful to have recognized that.

Since that time, I've worked with many people who didn't understand that synchronicities and signs reflect the way we're vibrating, which may or may not be in harmony with what we want. It is essential to discern how we *feel* about what's showing up, because our feelings let us know whether the sign is coming from our Expanded Self, or from a habit of thought that isn't in harmony with our genuine desires.

Making a call for guidance

Sometimes, on the path of saying *yes* to our desires, we have choices to make that aren't immediately clear. In my case, the decision about whether to sell my house was one of those choices. It made sense on paper, but of course, life isn't lived on paper. And I wanted to follow my heart, not the advice of others or my own scarcity-based conditioning.

Still, I wasn't clear about whether selling my home was the best way to finance my dreams. My heart was clear, but I had too much mental/emotional static in the way to recognize my heart's wisdom.

At one point, feeling impatient with myself for being so indecisive, I talked myself into selling my house and contacted a realtor. During our first visit, she assured me I was doing the right thing. I sat quietly at my kitchen table, listening to her and feeling very sad. One of her first steps was to arrange for a photographer to take pictures of my home that would be featured on her company's website. The day he showed up, my heart sank into the floor. I had experienced that sensation once before and ignored it, to disastrous effect. I wasn't going to make that mistake again.

I realized in that moment I simply could not sell my home. And so, I didn't. Shortly thereafter, in a moment of deep inner silence as I rested in child's pose, I felt warmth seep into my being as these simple thoughts came to me: "This house is my *home*. I belong here." That was the guidance I was looking for.

Much later, as I looked back on that experience, I realized that I had done something helpful in taking steps to sell my home, even though I didn't understand it at the time. It's what I now refer to as making a call for guidance. We "make the call" by taking small steps toward something we're considering—and checking in with ourselves at each step to see how it *feels*.

In general, the closer we get to something in our physical reality, the more readily we can sense our feelings about it. Often, just identifying the first step and imagining how we'll feel will yield the guidance we're looking for. If not, of course, then taking the step—or noticing our resistance to doing so—will help us find clarity.

Guidance that is hiding in plain view

Years ago, a student I'll call Linda participated in one of my early *Create the Work You Love* courses, which was a multi-part class series held over a period of weeks. Linda hoped the class would help her find the motivation to finish her master's thesis, which she hadn't touched in months. She was beating herself up for being lazy and unfocused.

Linda was a delightfully free spirit, and she admitted that what she really wanted to do was write a novel. Not understanding the tremendous value and power of her true desire, she told herself it was silly and that she should focus on completing her degree. I, of course, wanted her to see her desire differently. I was glad she had enrolled in the course.

As the course progressed, I learned that the topic of Linda's thesis was one that her romantic partner at the time, whom I'll call Tim, had suggested for her. Tim was a well-known, high-powered attorney in town, and Linda was thrilled that he was attracted to her. Deep down, she felt she wasn't good enough for Tim, and so she'd agreed to the topic he proposed, thinking it would increase his respect for her.

It was obvious to me, and finally to Linda, that her resistance to working on the thesis was her *guidance*. The thing she thought she wanted—to write her thesis on that topic—was a desire imposter and her resistance was letting her know that. With the enthusiastic support of her fellow students in the class, Linda gave herself permission to let the thesis go for a while and focus on what she genuinely wanted—and what she genuinely knew in her heart of hearts.

It turns out that Tim was both emotionally and physically abusive to Linda, and she needed to end the relationship. Happily, she did. Shortly after that, she got a job teaching creative writing at a nearby community college and absolutely loved it. I don't know if she ever wrote her novel, or if she found a new thesis topic and completed her degree. What I do know is that honoring her true desires and inner knowing, and walking away from the imposter desires, were the best and most loving things she could have done.

Resistance is always an invitation to slow down and go within, not to push through and overcome. The first question to ask ourselves is, "Am I resisting what I want, or resisting what I don't want?" And to give ourselves an honest answer.

If we discover we're resisting something we genuinely want to experience, that tells us our beliefs are not in harmony with our desire. We need to change our patterns of thought. We will continue to explore ways to do that, but a good question we can ask ourselves to get started is, "How might I love myself toward this desire?"

If we discover that we're resisting something we don't really want, which is our guidance to pause or stop what we're doing, we can practice *appreciating* the guidance and choosing to honor it. We might also, with loving curiosity, inquire within to discover why we might have said *yes* to something we didn't want.

As with any exploration of unhelpful beliefs, this is not meant to be a search-and-destroy mission. The idea here is to *allow* insights about false and painful beliefs to arise through our connection with our Expanded Self, not to dig for them out of frustration or impatience. When we see them for what they are, we can release them.

Often, like Linda, we say *yes* to things we don't really want, or have genuine interest in, thinking that we *should* do so for any number of reasons. At the core of those reasons is often a belief that we need to say *yes* so that people will like us—and beneath that is a fear that unwanted things will happen if we're not liked.

We have now reached a crucial point of understanding about guidance. Guidance from our Expanded Self, who is *always* in harmony with One Source, does not benefit us at the expense of others. That cannot be. All genuine guidance comes from the same place: One Source, which is, and can only ever be, in harmony with itself.

When we honor our individual guidance, we honor the Whole.

It may not always appear that way, at first. People who are disconnected from their Expanded Self may not be able to recognize the wisdom of choices made by those who are connected. In Linda's story, Tim was not at all pleased that she left the relationship. Yet it's clear that he could not grow beyond his own painfully false beliefs about life, which gave rise to his habit of demeaning and hurting women, with her continued participation in such an unhealthy dynamic. As Linda honored her guidance and ended the relationship, space was created in Tim's life, which in turn allowed for the possibility of change.

All transformative change is initiated in the space created when we suspend our usual habits of thought and action.

The arising of insight and realization

As we intentionally cultivate openness to receive guidance from our Expanded Self, we gain much more than guidance about specific steps we're taking, or options we're considering. We learn how to communicate with our Expanded Self and how to discern its true voice. Over time, we come into a live, interactive relationship with our Expanded Self, one that enhances and accelerates our understanding of who we really are—and who we are not.

Like Linda, we might discover we're in resistance to something because we thought we wanted it but, in truth, we do not—and we might want to ask ourselves why we said *yes* to it. Now I will expand on this by saying we might want to *ask our Expanded Self* why we said *yes* to it.

When we ask anything of our Expanded Self, we do so with the understanding that our only job is to ask, and to cultivate a state of mind and body that allows us to receive. We don't dig or force, guess or analyze. We relax; we release our Local Self thoughts about it, we open, and we receive. Answers may come in the moment we ask for them, or they may come later, when our minds are still and clear. We trust that whatever we need to know, we will know, in perfect timing.

Over time, we may not even need to ask questions about our misguided beliefs. Insights and realizations begin to arise spontaneously, as part of our ongoing connection with our Expanded Self. This has happened for me on many occasions as I reflected on–something I wanted to shift into a more loving, supportive direction.

Not long ago, I went through a period of intense frustration with some friends of mine, who were actively doing what I have committed *not* to do: they were blaming and condemning others who didn't see things the way they saw them. Their self-righteousness infuriated me, yet I knew, too, that in my infuriation I was vibrating with them. That was not who I wanted to be.

I couldn't have held a more sincere intention to shift my perspective about them. I began by asking myself what our situation was showing me that I wanted. I started writing about things such as mutual respect and listening. At some point, as I continued to reach for better-feeling thoughts in my journal, a realization came full-blown into my awareness. I suddenly saw the connection between *my* need to be "right"—in this case, being "right" about how "wrong" condemnation is—and my need to feel *safe*.

Growing up, I had been very afraid of my father's anger and wanted always to please him. The best way I knew how to do that was to do well in school, because that was of the utmost importance to him. Doing well in school meant getting good grades, and getting good grades was all about being "right" on tests. In my little girl mind, I had concluded that I had to be right to be safe.

That insight was tremendously liberating for me. In recognizing how profoundly false the belief was, I was able to begin releasing it. By that time, of course, I had come to understand that true safety can only be found through our union with One Source. I most certainly didn't "need" to be right to be safe; in fact, just the opposite is true. The need to be "right" arises only in separation consciousness, which is the level of consciousness from which our sense of vulnerability arises.

The insight also opened me to genuine compassion for my friends. I sensed that their own need to be "right" came from a similar false premise, most likely formed when they were afraid. I could extend my newfound compassion for myself to them, understanding that they had mistakenly but innocently believed something false to be true.

As profoundly helpful as that realization was for me, the point I want to make here is that *it came to me*, easily and gracefully. I didn't go looking for it. It came to me because I was exploring an experience I was living through in the present moment. I wasn't going back into my past to find out what belief I may have formed, and when, and why. My clear and abiding intention was to express who I wanted to be, *now*. As I continued to reach for thoughts that lifted me up, I came into vibrational range with my Expanded Self and that pivotal insight flowed into my awareness.

This is the beauty and benefit of cultivating a relationship with our Expanded Self. We don't have to work so hard to sort things out! We just need to maintain an ongoing commitment to bringing ourselves into vibrational range with our Expanded Self, so we can receive its precious wisdom.

Take a moment now to pause, breathe deeply and reflect on this chapter's Reflection Point:

Reflection Point
The clarity I need to make wise and loving choices is available through my relationship with my Expanded Self. The better I feel emotionally, the more open I am to receive its wisdom.

10

FLOWING WITH
THE PULSE OF LIFE

No work is required.
Tension and pain are not needed.
All movement of Love into Life is supported.
Know this and be free.

E verything just fell apart." My client, whom I'll call Frances, spoke quietly. She was describing a recent slowing down—it seemed more like an unraveling—that was occurring in the fledgling business she'd started about eighteen months prior to our meeting. She wasn't sure what to do and, even if she had been sure, she didn't have the energy to move forward. She felt lost, frustrated, and exhausted.

But everything was not falling apart. It was finding a way back to its natural rhythm and readying itself for the next wave of expansion. It was evolving.

Life in this endlessly creative, energy-based Universe is all about growth, change, and evolution. Although we often impose linear, goal-oriented processes and timelines on our human endeavors, Life itself is circular, cyclical, and organic. Growth occurs in phases that are governed by the way energy operates, which is in waves or pulses.

Desire is the impetus for growth. It is the impulse of One Source—Love— to continually express and experience itself in new ways, which creates Life. So, we may think of desire as the pulse of Life itself.

This creative Life Pulse has four distinct, recurring phases: inner stasis, expansion, outer stasis, and contraction. This is reflected in the rhythm of our breath, the ebb and flow of the ocean tides, and the changing seasons of nature.

It can also be recognized in the experience of a creative project, which originates in the stillness of saying *yes* to a desire (inner stasis), moves outward through action (expansion), pauses at completion to be acknowledged, celebrated, and experienced (outer stasis), then is followed by a period of reflection on and integration of all that was learned—and all that is newly desired (contraction). Returning to inner stasis, we connect deeply with ourselves to replenish, to honor what we've learned, and to become clear about the *yes* that will initiate the next round of expansion.

Or at least, that's how it goes when we move with the pulse of Life. When we don't—when we do not recognize or understand the Life Pulse—we miss the subtle clues about what phase we are in. We expect things to progress in a predictable, linear way, and we get frustrated when they don't. We criticize ourselves when we aren't being "productive." We worry that things aren't moving forward according to plan.

As we introduce fear and judgment into the creative process—fear of not finishing soon enough, let's say, or judgment that we're not moving quickly enough—the natural cycle is distorted. We push ourselves into new phases of expansion before the current cycle has been completed, then we exhaust ourselves and collapse directly into inner stasis rather than enjoying the fertile contraction time of integration and reflection.

What could be an experience of being in the flow is, instead, an experience of struggle and frustration. It's like the difference between breathing easily and effortlessly when you're relaxed and gasping for air when you've pushed your body too hard while exercising. One feels natural. The other feels like you're dying.

Learning to recognize and honor the pulse of Life gets you back in the flow. It's partnering with Life rather than pushing against it. It teaches you to value all phases of the creative process, and in doing so it allows you to experience the fullness of your own creativity. You begin to experience greater ease and less struggle.

In Frances's case, the first expansion phase of her new venture was a big one. The business ramped up quickly, which suited her high-energy, action-oriented personality perfectly. As with any entrepreneur, she was learning a lot of new things all at once, in diverse areas. She learned everything from how to assemble a board of directors to how to get marketing support at an affordable price to how to ensure new team members got the training they needed.

Because she was new to both entrepreneurship and the thought /emotion energy dynamic, and because she'd never heard of the Life Pulse, she ignored her body's need for rest. She tolerated uncomfortable emotions such as frustration and impatience, not realizing that they were signals for her to pause and redirect her focus.

As action oriented as she was, and wanting to generate immediate results, Frances believed she had to "make things happen," and kept pushing herself to do so. She did not intentionally slow down for the deep inner connection with her Expanded Self that might have provided helpful insights and guidance.

She enjoyed an early string of successes before the unraveling began. Key employees in essential roles turned out not to be a good fit. Hoped-for investors fell through. Friction with the landlord became evident.

From the perspective of expecting things to keep moving forward at a rapid pace, it appeared as if everything was falling apart. From the perspective of the creative Life Pulse, she was being redirected to experience all its essential phases. She had been trying to extend the expansion phase, but it was time to pause and acknowledge herself for all she had learned and created so far. It was time to review and assess things. It was time to let go of what wasn't working and ask new questions about how things might be done differently. It was time to get clear about desires and priorities. It was also time to rest, replenish, and get ready for the next phase of expansion.

Like Frances, many of us have been conditioned to value only the expansion phase of the Life Pulse, which means we deprive ourselves of the immense benefits of the other phases. Let's look more closely at each phase of the Life Pulse as it relates to the manifestation of desire.

Inner stasis

This is an inner-focused phase from which the next expansion phase originates. It is the point at which we say *yes* to a desire, effectively setting the intention to manifest it. Ideally, our *yes* arises from a clear mind and an open heart, having at least begun to cultivate a consciousness that is in harmony with the desire during the concentration phase immediately preceding inner stasis.

Like all phases of the Life Pulse, the experience of inner stasis and the amount of time we spend in that phase varies widely, in accordance with our personalities and preferences and with the nature of the growth cycle we're in. For some, it can be experienced in a single, simple moment of deciding to do a particular thing that we genuinely want to do. For others, it can be an extended period of deep inner connection, such as we experience during a silent retreat, with the intention of discovering the desire awaiting our *yes*.

The amount of time we spend in inner stasis, and the frequency with which we return to it, reflect our unique rhythms. Regardless of its duration in any cycle, the essence of inner stasis is deep inner connection with our Expanded Self and a feeling of equilibrium. We are at peace.

Expansion

This is an outer-focused phase of action. By maintaining a steady focus on our desire, staying emotionally close to how we feel, making course corrections as needed, and creating time on a regular basis for deep inner listening, we are inspired with ideas and impulses that move us forward. We are graced with synchronistic meetings and opportunities that find their way easily to us. We enjoy the unfolding of our desire from idea to physical manifestation.

This is the phase that many of us have been conditioned to equate with productivity and success, although we don't always experience expansion the way I've described it. Like Frances, we believe we're supposed to be actively pursuing our goals almost all the time. The key to riding this phase of the pulse with ease and grace is staying close to ourselves and our desires so that our actions are genuine, inspired, and efficient rather than forced and exhausting.

Outer stasis

This is an outer-focused phase in which we experience the results of our manifestation, whether they are a brief moment in time, such as graduation day after completing four years of college, or many years in length, such as continuing to enjoy a wonderful job we manifested. It is a time for acknowledgment, appreciation, and celebration of what we have created and how we have grown. It is also a new level of experience from which we can identify fresh desires.

The essence of outer statis is one of genuine connection with others. It is an integration of our personal creation with the larger tapestry of All That Is. It is a necessary and stable pause between the expansion and contraction phases that allows us to balance our inner and outer focus with the new experience we've created.

Outer stasis is where we live much of the time. It's the steady state, the normal routines of our careers, relationships, health practices, and other

161

areas of our lives. It's easy to drift into autopilot in this phase, which is why it continues to be essential to stay close to ourselves, so we can detect the subtle shifts in our energy, preferences, and desires that signal a shift to the next phase. Feelings of boredom or restlessness are often a signal that a desire for something different is emerging.

Contraction

This is an inner-focused phase during which we look within ourselves to review where we are and what we've learned, to clarify what we want, and to cultivate thought patterns to support it. I often refer to this phase as the concentration phase because we concentrate our focus very intentionally during this phase to create energetic momentum for the next phase of expansion. (Remember, energy follows attention.)

This is also the phase during which we acknowledge, feel, and shift any uncomfortable feelings that may have been activated. These feelings may have been activated if the new desire, which prompted us to shift from outer stasis to contraction, was stimulated by something unwanted. Uncomfortable feelings could also be activated by any false or limiting thoughts we have about our new desire, regardless of how the desire, itself, was stimulated. Depending on the nature of the new desire and the degree of change it will create in our lives, this phase can take a few minutes or several years or any amount of time in between.

This inward-focused phase of contraction seems to be the most difficult one for people to embrace, most likely because we've been conditioned to value only the expansion phase of the creative process. When we're not in action mode, we judge ourselves as stagnant or lazy, and that judgment is very painful. More generally, this phase is often uncomfortable because many people haven't learned to love themselves through life. They resist going within because, when they do, their tendency is to find fault with themselves. So, we must maintain an ongoing intention for kindness and compassion as we review where we are and what we now want.

It is helpful and important to understand that the contraction phase is not the same thing as resistance. The natural contraction, or turning inward, of this phase takes our focus away from what we're currently experiencing so that we can concentrate on what is newly desired. Through our consistent inner focus on what is wanted, the Law of Attraction responds by bringing us more thoughts to support it, until we've strengthened and stabilized those thoughts to the point where manifestation can occur. In this way, the contraction phase *creates* flow. Resistance—which is focused in *opposition* to what is wanted—blocks it.

The contraction phase doesn't need to be the same length or duration as the expansion phase. It simply takes the time *we* need to concentrate our thought patterns into harmony with our desires. Taking the time to do so before jumping into major action benefits us enormously and is often completely overlooked.

Giving ourselves time to identify and cultivate a consciousness that supports our desires sets us up to experience a delicious phase of inner stasis, as we allow ourselves to relish the high-vibration, good-feeling place of being in harmony with the desire to which we're saying *yes*. It also paves the way for a satisfying and ease-filled expansion phase because, having developed positive expectations of realizing our desire, we won't be pushing against our own doubting thoughts. And in our good-feeling place of positive expectation we can more easily tune into the inner guidance that prompts our effective action.

This isn't to imply that we should take *no* action toward our desires until and unless we've formed air-tight patterns of thought that disallow any false or limiting beliefs. That isn't necessary or even possible. We often experience genuine impulses to do certain things quickly, especially if a new desire is strongly felt and very inspiring to us. It's helpful to act on those impulses, to continue building momentum.

And we can't even recognize—until we're in the expansion phase—the subtle nuances of thought about our desire that we want to shift. The process of cultivating a consciousness to support our desires is an ongoing one, applicable to all phases of the Life Pulse. It's why we need to stay close to how we're feeling each step of the way, so we readily become aware when shifts are needed.

What I want to emphasize is that we can give ourselves a loving head start on the process by taking time during the contraction phase to recognize how helpful or unhelpful our current thinking is with respect to our desire, and to begin shifting it toward the helpful end of the spectrum. That way we're less likely to manifest unwanted things that reflect the unhelpful thoughts, making our experience easier.

Finally, it is important to understand that the contraction phase doesn't take us "back to square one." It concentrates energy for the next wave of expansion *from where we are*. The expansion of All That Is, is eternal.

Cycles upon cycles and cycles within cycles

Although these phases of the Life Pulse are distinct from one another in terms of their purpose and direction of focus (outer or inner), we move through all of them, every day, in all areas of our lives. Everything we experience is ebbing and flowing with the pulse of Life, including our health, our careers, our spirituality, and our relationships. Just as the various aspects of our physical bodies have their own rhythms—our breath, our heartrate, our cycles of sleeping and waking—each aspect of our life has its own rhythm.

For example, we may be in outer stasis with respect to the job we've had for several years, while at the same time being in the contraction phase with respect to our health after being diagnosed with an illness.

Also, there are cycles within cycles. For example, if we're in the expansion phase of starting a new business, we benefit ourselves greatly by establishing frequent, regular practices (such as meditation) that call us inward for clarity, replenishment, and guidance. Those practices effectively generate mini pulses of contraction and inner stasis, within the overall arc of an expansion phase. They help us stay in harmony with our desires, which is essential to a smooth expansion phase.

Likewise, we often experience mini pulses of expansion while we're in the contraction phase, such as when we try different things to assess whether or not they are a good fit for us.

As an example, imagine that you have just broken up with your partner of several years, which signals the end of an outer stasis phase and the beginning of a contraction phase. You turn inward to feel your feelings and get curious about who you are and what you want, now. Not being entirely sure, you "make a call for guidance" by joining a dating site and going on a few dates, to learn firsthand what kind of person feels resonant with you now. Each date is its own mini cycle of expansion—focusing outward and connecting with others—within the larger phase of contraction with respect to creating a new primary relationship.

Fundamentally, the Life Pulse is a continuous flow from the inner to the outer, over and over, again and again. The rhythm and duration of its cycles vary widely, depending on the nature of what is being created. We experience long cycles in all areas of our lives whose phases extend over multiple days, months, or years, yet within those phases are mini cycles of all the phases.

Writing a book is an excellent example of this dynamic. Each chapter has multiple cycles of the Life Pulse as it moves from concept to first draft and through the editing and rewriting process toward its final form. The writer experiences all four phases, even though she remains in the expansion phase with respect to the book as a whole.

The feel of the Life Pulse

Our emotions are the best indicator of whether we're flowing with the Life Pulse or have gotten out of sync with it. In general, there are two ways we can experience being out of sync:

We take actions that are consistent with the phase of the Life Pulse we're in, yet we experience uncomfortable emotions. This tells us our thought patterns are not in harmony with the phase we're in, or with our desires.

The Life Pulse has shifted to a new phase—for example, from expansion to outer stasis—but we're not aware of it and keep doing what we've been doing. Eventually, being out of sync will generate some kind of uncomfortable feeling, which is the signal to shift focus.

An example of the first situation is when the Life Pulse is in the active expansion phase, and we are as well. Yet we're feeling exhausted rather than exhilarated. This means we've got thoughts related to what we're doing that are not in harmony with the Life Pulse, such as, "I've got to get this done *now*," or "I am so far behind," and we're acting on those thoughts and pushing ourselves to take action rather than acting when the energy is there for the action.

An example of the second situation is when we've reached an interim milestone at the end of its expansion phase and it's time to pause, acknowledge, appreciate, and fully experience where we are—in outer stasis—but we do not. Instead, we think something such as, "I'm not there yet," and we march forward. We miss the *enjoyment* of having created what we've created so far, which is deeply nourishing. We also miss the opportunity that would arise from following outer stasis into the contraction or concentration phase, which is to assess where we are and see if any new desires or preferences have arisen that might indicate a course correction.

Being in flow with the Life Pulse is supposed to feel good! Below is a simple chart that identifies the types of feelings we naturally feel when we're in harmony with it.

Life Pulse Phase	Feelings
Inner stasis	Peaceful
	Clear
	Still
	Trusting
Expansion	Inspired
	Exhilarated
	Enthusiastic
	Eager
	Focused
Outer stasis	Content
	Appreciative
	Balanced
	Engaged
Contraction	Contemplative
	Attentive to our inner thoughts and feelings
	Reflective
	Open, exploratory

Although each person's experience of being in harmony with the Life Pulse is unique to them, this gives you a general sense of how good the Life Pulse is meant to feel as it flows through you.

Flowing into manifestation

Let's look at a real-life example of how flowing with the Life Pulse, rather than ignoring or pushing against it, can yield absolutely delightful results. One of my clients, whom I'll call Theresa, had worked at the same company for many years. She was in the outer stasis phase of the Life Pulse. The job suited her schedule and temperament, but over time a new desire emerged for something more fulfilling and better suited to her skills and talents, with a company whose values more closely matched her own.

Right around that time, her company merged with another company and Theresa was laid off. This was the start of a new phase of the Life Pulse, the contraction phase, and it's where many people fail to make the turn inward to stay on the wave. Often, like Frances in the earlier story I shared, they keep pushing outward.

In Theresa's case, had she not been as familiar with the Life Pulse as she was, she might have done what so many others do when something unwanted or unexpected occurs. She might have jumped right into action by updating her resume, reaching out to network contacts, and scouring job boards.

Instead, Theresa turned inward, as the contraction phase calls us to do. She needed to acknowledge her feelings of hurt and anger at having been laid off, and to very intentionally find a perspective that felt better. In truth, she already knew what the better-feeling perspective was. She understood that the merger and subsequent layoff was a manifestation that reflected what she truly wanted, which was to leave that company and find a better job. But her hurt feelings were creating vibrational static that prevented her from fully embracing that perspective.

And so, Theresa acknowledged her uncomfortable feelings with compassion, nudging herself toward thoughts that were supportive of her talents and desires, rather than thoughts of how unfairly she felt she was treated. She also took the time to reflect on what she really wanted in her next job.

Just as important was what she chose *not* to do. She chose not to push herself to update her resume and social media profiles, or reach out to her network contacts, until she had the genuine energy and willingness to do so. Instead, she went on vacation with her family and had a glorious time. She returned, filled with appreciation for the experience and feeling much more grounded and energized than she had before she left. She felt clear about what she wanted and ready to say *yes* to it, believing she could manifest it.

I don't remember the exact timing of what happened next, but I know it was swift. Shortly after returning from vacation and saying that inner *yes* to the kind of job she really wanted, Theresa was contacted by someone she knew who wanted her to interview for a position in his company. The position was ideal for Theresa. A new expansion phase had begun, and it was a fast one. The interview process went exceptionally well, and Theresa was hired for the job. She was ecstatic, and I was delighted.

What an elegant manifestation! This is what can happen when we flow with the Life Pulse rather than push against it. I'm sure Theresa updated her resume as part of the interview process, but other than that, she did not push through her uncomfortable feelings and take the usual steps to "get" a job. It literally came to her, because the Life Pulse, itself—the pulse of desire—brought it to her.

The pulse of creation

Essentially, the Life Pulse is a way of understanding the creative process: the movement of desire from the inner to the outer and back again, over and over in endless, rhythmic waves. These opposite directions of movement are complementary aspects of the same dynamic. They both prompt and reflect each other, and as feedback from one cycle feeds into the next, the evolution of desire—and the expansion of the Universe—occurs.

As we consider the eternal expansion of the Universe, it becomes clear that the realization of any desire automatically becomes the new "farthest edge" of All That Is, which then serves as a limit to be transcended or a platform of fresh diversity from which new desires emerge. This ongoing expansion doesn't have to be an expansion into "more" in terms of quantity. It can be expansion into new or deeper types of experience.

Looking at this through the experience of an individual, imagine that you have established yourself as a business coach, and you've just gone through an expansion phase that has doubled the number of clients you serve. As you experience this new level of activity in outer stasis, a fresh desire for administrative support might emerge. Turning inward to reflect on this new desire and say *yes* to it, a new expansion phase is initiated, and you are guided into the actions and opportunities that bring your ideal assistant to you.

Your business continues to grow, as does the support you need to sustain it. At some point you might reach an outer stasis threshold of success from which you no longer desire more clients, but rather more private time for deep self-connection. This represents an expansion into a different dimension of experience.

Letting it work for you

You are on a magnificent journey of awakening to more and more of who you are, through the conscious honoring of your genuine desires. These desires pulse with the intelligence and power required for their realization. As you deepen your understanding and felt sense of the Life Pulse, you begin to relax and feel more at ease in your life. Rather than assuming that things are going "wrong" when they're not proceeding according to your plan, and rather than ignoring or pushing yourself through uncomfortable feelings, you ask yourself what phase of the Life Pulse you're in and choose to follow its lead.

For example, if you feel frustrated by a seeming lack of progress in some area of your life, you may be in outer stasis and resisting the natural contraction phase of the Life pulse, which is ready to take place. Take time to review and reflect and consider what you need to let go of and what you might want to do differently. Most importantly, ask yourself what fresh desires are emerging that you may not yet have acknowledged.

If you feel bored or restless, you may have stayed a bit too long in inner stasis, and the Life Pulse is prompting you into a new phase of expansion that you've been resisting. This is more likely to occur with introverts, who relish the inner-focused phases of the Life Pulse and feel less comfortable in the outer-focused ones. Pause and go deeply within. Honor yourself wherever you are and ask for guidance about what is now ready to emerge.

If you've just reached a beautiful milestone or accomplished something you feel good about, please take the time to acknowledge, appreciate and celebrate it! Don't just keep marching toward the next milestone. Follow the lead of the Life Pulse and let it carry you, with ease and grace, into your next cycle of experience.

Let me suggest two areas of exploration to help you tune into your Life Pulse:

Consider your life as a whole and ask yourself this question: do I generally experience all four phases of the Life Pulse, or do I tend to stay in one or two of them? If the latter is true for you, get curious! Might it be time to move to the next phase?

In general, do your best to take action only it falls into *all* of the following categories:

It is an *authentic* impulse, not a "should." It feels inspired, or your intuitive feeling about it is, "This is mine to do"—not out of obligation, but from a sense of "rightness."

You're genuinely *willing* to do it now.

You have the *energy*, in this moment, to do it.

Focus a little less on getting lots of things done and more on how you're thinking about yourself and your life. Keep nudging yourself toward loving and supportive thoughts.

Understanding and flowing with the Life Pulse opens you to greater ease, fulfillment, and enjoyment as you expand into your magnificence. Remember, you didn't come here to prove your worthiness. You came here to express it and celebrate it!

Reflection Point

The energy of pure desire pulses with the power and momentum of Life itself. This Life Pulse has natural phases of expansion, contraction, and stasis. As I learn to recognize and honor each phase, my life flows with ease and grace.

PART THREE

Applying the Principles

11

THE FOUR PORTALS OF TRANSFORMATION

Hold your desires lightly but with steady hands.

I lay on my living room floor, relishing how good I felt after a particularly expansive meditation. As I breathed softly, the gentle yet electrifying *ping* of a new realization made its presence known in my mind. Although it didn't come through in words, its meaning was immediately clear to me.

I realized that the manifestation of our desires is far easier than is generally understood. There is a lightness and naturalness to desire, yet also an inherent potency that is self-fulfilling. Everything I want *already exists* within my Expanded Self, waiting to be expressed. My desires are not separate from who I am. They are expressions *of* who I am, just as I am an expression of One Source. My desires exist *because I do*. They are real and ready to live through me, as me. I don't need to make them happen, I just need to relax and let them in.

I felt liberated and more joyfully at peace than ever before. I understood that the journey of waking up to the glorious truth of who we are is one of trusting the inherent goodness of Life and the life-giving nature of desire. It all seemed so simple, logical, and ingenious.

Only later did I ask the question you may be asking yourself right now: If it's so easy, why does it often seem so hard?

The answer is that we don't understand how it all works when we're in separation consciousness, where so much of humanity lives. We don't understand *who we are*. We construct habits of thought from false premises about who we are and what is possible for us to experience. And those habits of thought make things hard for us.

The transition from habits of thought that aren't in harmony with our pure desires to ones that are isn't a process as much as it is an exploration. There are no maps or formulas to follow. There are techniques and practices to experiment with as you open to greater awareness of what you genuinely want and how your guidance communicates with you. As you are better able to get out of your own way and into the flow of your desires, you will continually strengthen the thought patterns that are harmonious with what you want. As those thought patterns stabilize, the ease, grace, and joy you have longed to experience become your reality.

In this chapter and the next, I want to share with you several of the techniques and practices that have been helpful to my clients and me over the years. Trust your intuition to help you recognize those that are likely to be of greatest benefit to you. Dive in with the spirit of an explorer on a wondrous adventure, and experiment with creating your own practices and techniques as you go along.

The time it takes for this exploration to yield sustainable results may be longer than you would prefer it to be. Do your best to suspend all thoughts about timetables and intend to love yourself through the explorations, moment by moment, looking for ways to enjoy the exploration itself. It is, after all, your life.

The four portals of transformation

The journey of waking up to who we are is one of transformation. As our awareness expands, we transform our self-identity, our patterns of thought and our lived experiences. These transformations occur through any or all of what I call the four portals of transformation:

Awareness

Intention

Willingness

Practice

All the techniques and practices I offer intentionally utilize these portals. They are intimately intertwined with each other, yet each has a distinct purpose.

Awareness

As awareness of both our inner and outer world expands, we perceive new things, or we perceive the same things differently. These new perceptions give rise to new understandings, new questions, and new desires. In the absence of new desires, transformation does not occur.

Intention

Desire is the very heart of intention. We would not intend anything if we didn't want it. As new desires arise in our minds and hearts and we say *yes* to them, they become intentions.

Willingness

The manifestation of a new desire requires that we develop new habits of thought that allow it to manifest in our physical experience. To flow with the Life Pulse rather than push against it, we call on willingness to develop those new habits of thought, rather than forcing ourselves to do so. Willingness has the same clear, strong energy as willpower—*will*—but it is guided by love rather than coercion.

Practice

Although near-instant transformations of thought can occur during an extraordinary experience of expanded awareness (such as a near-death experience), practice is generally required to strengthen and stabilize new habits of thought. They must become our dominant thoughts to yield desired manifestations.

To state it simply: from a place of expanded awareness that gives rise to new desires, we intentionally call upon our willingness to practice new habits of thought, or new perspectives, which allow the new desires to flow into our experience.

The practices offered in this chapter are what I think of as day-to-day practices. In the next chapter, I will offer practices and exercises that utilize the power of the written or spoken word, as well as nonverbal imagery. Both types of practices are beneficial. I encourage you to experiment with them and modify them in any way that feels good to you.

Practices to develop emotional awareness and vibrational mastery

Become more aware of how you feel

How you feel is an indicator of whether you're moving toward or away from your desires. Therefore, it is highly beneficial to become more keenly aware of your current emotional range and your current "go-to" emotions. This starts with an intention to do so, and a willingness to believe that you can develop more finely tuned sensitivity to your own feelings.

To get started, ask yourself these questions:

How do I feel generally about life?

How do I feel generally about this subject? (i.e., any particular area of your life)

How do I feel in this moment?

As you reflect on your answers to these questions, note whether there is a relationship between how you feel and what types of manifested experiences are consistently showing up in your life. The simple table below may be helpful. It identifies four categories of emotions and what they reveal about your momentum toward or away from what is wanted.

Type of emotion	Yes or No to desire	Energy movement
Sad, depressed	Disconnected	No energy moving
Angry, blaming	No	Negative momentum
Bored, irritated	Yes and No	Paralysis, back and forth
Happy, joyful	Yes	Positive momentum

See if you can identify which of the four categories your answers to the questions fall into. For example, if you answered the first question with, "I feel really good," that likely falls into the happy or joyful category, and you're likely manifesting things you enjoy on a regular basis. If you answered the second question with, "I don't give a damn," that would likely fall into the bored or irritated category, and you may be experiencing a mix of things you want and things you don't want in almost equal amounts in that area of your life.

If there doesn't appear to be a relationship between how you feel and what is showing up in your life, it's likely that you're not fully sensitive to what you're actually feeling. Many of us have been conditioned to ignore or suppress our feelings, and we've also become so accustomed to stressful feelings that we consider them normal. The following simple exercise can help you regain or further enhance your ability to detect nuances of emotion.

Commit to checking in with yourself regularly throughout the day for the express purpose of identifying how you feel. Simply pause and ask yourself these two questions:

How do I feel?

What was I just thinking?

Do not analyze or criticize your feelings, just note them and their relationship to your thoughts.

A wonderful alchemy occurs when you take a little time to regularly acknowledge your feelings and observe the relationship between feelings and thoughts. This act of self-acknowledgment, done with acceptance rather than judgment, fortifies your sense of self-worth. It moves you toward the vibrational range of your Expanded Self, and you begin to adjust your thoughts toward ones that feel better without overthinking them. You begin to understand that you are worthy of feeling good.

After doing this for a while, perhaps a week or two, you will be able to sense your feelings more readily *as they arise*, not just when you check in. This is tremendously helpful, because the sooner you recognize an uncomfortable feeling, which means the sooner you recognize you're moving away from what you want, the sooner you can make a course correction with whatever practice is most helpful in that moment.

Regarding those course corrections, know that it is virtually impossible to make *big* shifts in how you feel in any given moment. It is unlikely, for example, that you could shift from depression to joy in a matter of minutes or even hours, because the vibrational frequencies are so vastly different. So, don't demand that of yourself. Keep intending to stay close to how you feel, and to move yourself toward feeling better.

Identify and practice the feelings you want to feel

Remember that emotions are always associated with thoughts, *even if those thoughts aren't expressed in words.* Emotions reveal how we're interpreting things, what meaning we're giving them, even if we haven't yet articulated that interpretation. So, every emotion *means something.* What any given emotion means can vary from person to person, but within a person a given emotion usually has a consistent or similar meaning, from topic to topic.

Here are some examples of what emotions might mean, if translated into words:

Depression: "I have nothing to live for."

Anger: "This is wrong."

Frustration: "Nothing is ever easy for me."

Satisfaction: "I am right where I want to be."

Optimism: "I have so much to look forward to!"

Delight: "Life is wonderful."

With this understanding, we can call on emotions to help us fortify thought patterns that support our desires. For example, the more I cultivate the feeling of delight in my life, the more I strengthen its underlying thought that life is wonderful. And the stronger that thought is, the more readily anything I want can flow into my experience.

Here are two ways to bring any desired feeling into your experience:

Evoke the feeling intentionally. This can be done in many ways, including meditation, listening to uplifting music, gazing at inspiring art, spending time in nature, moving your body in ways that feel good, consciously choosing to remember the feeling, or simply asking yourself, "How do I

181

want to feel?" and then reaching for that feeling as you identify it. However you evoke a desired feeling, stay with it as long as you can, and acknowledge how good and natural it feels.

Decide you're going to feel a particular way more often in your life. Ask your Expanded Self, "How might I experience more _____?" Keep the question open for a while—think about it, meditate on it, talk about it with a loved one, draw or paint the feeling, journal about it, or do anything enjoyable that helps you connect with it. Incorporate activities you associate with the feeling into your life on a regular basis.

Two feelings in particular can easily and powerfully move you into vibrational harmony with your Expanded Self: appreciation and satisfaction. When these feelings become common in your experience, so many things start to flow easily that you naturally begin to hold positive expectations about all areas of your life. They effectively jumpstart momentum toward all that fulfills you.

And what's wonderful about them is that they are easy to cultivate. There is always something that can be appreciated in every day, and the more you look for things to appreciate, the easier they will be to find. I especially encourage you to look for qualities to appreciate in *yourself.*

Many people have gratitude practices, which is a feeling similar to appreciation. I prefer the feeling of appreciation to that of gratitude because appreciation is *pure.* When you feel appreciation, you are basking in whatever you enjoy or respect or like or are inspired by. With gratitude, there is often a vibrational reference to something unwanted that was avoided. There can be a feeling of, "Whew! So glad I dodged that bullet" or perhaps, "There, but for the grace of God, go I."

Even if the vibrational reference isn't that strong or obvious, people often express gratitude after moving through a difficult time, or out of relief that something that could have gone wrong did not. The unwanted is still fresh in the mind and therefore active in vibration. And so, I encourage you to focus on feeling appreciation, rather than gratitude, as often and as deeply as you can.

Like appreciation, satisfaction is easy to cultivate. Even things we may not enjoy doing, such as working on our tax returns, can be opportunities to find satisfaction when we make progress—as long as we *intend* to find satisfaction. So, I encourage you to intend to find satisfaction in as many of your daily activities as you can and be willing to be surprised by how easy it is.

Also, play with the feeling of satisfaction as you do things you truly enjoy, such as eating a wonderful meal. Say out loud, "That was so *satisfying*." And feel it! The more often and the more strongly you feel any good-feeling emotion, the more you strengthen and stabilize its associated thought pattern.

Allowing unwanted feelings to be felt

If an uncomfortable emotion is triggered powerfully or suddenly within you, you're likely to experience intense emotional static, and you are not able to access the kinds of thoughts your Expanded Self is holding about whatever is upsetting you.

Much like an adrenaline surge that is triggered by something fearful, an emotional surge must be allowed to complete its cycle. Attempting to interrupt or block it will only serve to keep the emotion active, perhaps vibrating less intensely but still not resolved. And so, the wisest thing you can do is to allow the wave of emotion to flow through you, unimpeded, until it comes to shore and then recedes on its own.

The key to doing this successfully and lovingly is to suspend all thought and place your attention in your *body*, where the emotion can be most strongly felt. If you continue to think about what upset you, the emotion continues to ramp up. Shifting your focus from the thoughts that triggered the emotion to the *emotion itself*, vibrating in your body, requires a very deliberate intention. Making that shift is the most challenging aspect of this practice, but I guarantee it is well worth practicing.

Once you've shifted your focus into your body, where you can feel the emotion, invite your heart to open as you bring your breathing into a steadier rhythm. You may want to repeat the phrase, "Breathe and feel, breathe and feel," either silently or aloud, to reduce the likelihood of your mind going back to the painful thoughts. Genuinely intend to experience how this emotion *feels*—perhaps heavy, or hot, or prickly, or dense, or any other quality of feeling you can detect. Imagine or sense the emotion as energy, pulsing or vibrating in its unique way.

Say *yes* to the emotion, over and over, as you experience it. This is an aspect of your life force energy, your vitality! Trying to make it go away would only leave you feeling depleted. You're saying yes to the *energy* of the emotion, not to the painful thoughts that gave rise to it.

At some point, as you continue breathing and feeling and saying *yes*, the emotion will shift or subside. You may still be able to feel it, but you sense that this process is complete for the moment. Acknowledge and appreciate yourself for having responded to your uncomfortable emotion in such a wise and loving way, then gently but firmly direct your focus to something other than whatever stimulated the emotional response. Anything that feels neutral or better is what you're looking for.

Commit to feeling as good as you can, as often as you can

As a general and ongoing intention, choose to feel as good as you can, as often as you can. As you cultivate feelings such as satisfaction, delight, optimism, peace, contentment, and joy, you activate the thought patterns that are associated with those feelings. Those thought patterns, of course, are in harmony with your Expanded Self, and therefore with your desires.

You may remember the client I called Jessica, who focused on cultivating peace. In doing so, she shifted from a life that felt constricted, unsafe, and worrisome to one that feels expansive, loving, and joyful. She allowed her

Expanded Self to surprise her with things she hadn't been fully aware she wanted or liked.

In the cultivation of peace, she activated peaceful thoughts. As they became stronger and her life began flowing with greater ease, she became more trusting in the goodness of Life. And as her trust deepened, she continued to experience more fun and fulfillment in all areas of her life.

I think of this as *surrendered* manifesting. We make a conscious choice to cultivate the feeling state in which we want to live, and then we surrender to our belief in the goodness of Life and our worthiness to receive the good that Life has to offer. As we do so, we come into greater vibrational harmony with our Expanded Self and all that we desire, whether we're consciously aware of what we desire or not. Life keeps getting better and better.

With surrendered manifestation, we're not focusing on specific things or experiences we desire. We simply trust that whatever comes our way will be joyful, satisfying, or beneficial in some way. This is an absolutely beautiful way to live. Another beautiful way to live is what I refer to as *empowered* manifesting. This is when we have clear desires for things or experiences, and we deliberately bring our thoughts into harmony with them so they can manifest in our lives. My friend Joy's manifestation of the beautiful cottage is an example of empowered manifesting.

Neither manifesting experience is better than the other, and we can choose to experience both of them. What they have in common is the commitment to lifting our vibration, which means finding loving and creative ways to feel as good as we can feel, as often as we can.

Toward this end, I encourage you to become very mindful of what you're allowing to influence the way you think and, therefore, the way you feel. Consider the information you take in from news and social media, the people with whom you interact and the nature of the conversations you have, the blogs you read and the podcasts and music you listen to, and any other source. In other words, consider the nature of thoughts you are consuming, the way you might consider the quality of food you're eating.

Are they uplifting, or inspiring, or helpful, or affirming, or expansive, or joyful? Or might they be alarming, or depressing, or mean-spirited, or caustic, or righteous, or hateful? Is their focus generally on solutions and what is wanted, or is their focus on problems and what is unwanted? Do you feel better or worse after consuming them?

It *is* necessary for us to recognize and acknowledge what we don't want, so we can more clearly identify what we *do* want. But in general, the focus of our news media and many of our cultural conversations is predominantly on what is wrong and needs to be fixed, rather than on what is going well and how we might create more of what we want. A relentless focus on what is "wrong" or "bad" can leave us feeling angry, depressed, and disempowered.

Remember, your personal, Local Self consciousness is contributing to humanity's collective consciousness. When you're vibrating powerfully with things you want such as peace, harmony, creativity and respect, you're strengthening those same vibrations in the collective consciousness. And the stronger they become, the more readily others' vibrations can be attuned to those frequencies.

You matter, what you want matters and how you feel matters. Know that you are worthy of feeling good in your life, and commit to feeling as good as you can, as often as you can. It is the ultimate win-win scenario. Everyone benefits.

Honor your authentic impulses, willingness, and energy

This is a practice I created to help me get into harmony with the Life Pulse. It's simple yet subtly and powerfully effective. I introduced it in chapter ten and want to expand on it here as an ongoing practice.

The practice is simply to choose what to do, and when, based on three criteria:

The impulse to do it is *authentic*.

You are genuinely *willing* to do it now.

You have the *energy* to do it now.

These criteria are related to each other, yet each is distinct. All three must be met before taking action.

An authentic impulse is one that is meaningful or valuable to you, something you desire or prefer, or a spontaneous idea that feels neutral or better. Most importantly, it is not a "should." It isn't something you force yourself to do because you're afraid that if you don't something unwanted will occur. Nor is it something you force yourself to do because you have judged yourself lazy and needing to be pushed into action to accomplish things. Fear and judgment may get you moving, but they will never get you happy.

An authentic impulse could be anything—cleaning your bathroom, working on your tax return, going to a favorite boutique on the spur of the moment, returning phone calls, applying for a job you've been considering, reading an entire book all in one sitting, or taking a nap. The key is how it feels. If it feels like a should, it's not authentic. If it feels like a good idea right now, it is.

At first, determining whether an impulse is authentic is challenging, conditioned as we've been to making lists of everything we think we need to do, and then working our way down the list. Be lighthearted about it—no analyzing or overthinking allowed—but be intentional about developing the discernment required to recognize what is authentic to you. When in doubt, use the remaining two criteria as your guide. If you have the willingness *and* energy to do it now, go ahead and do it.

If you have more than one authentic impulse in a given moment, and the energy and willingness to do any of them, choose the one that is most enjoyable or appealing.

Occasionally, you may benefit from nudging or coaxing yourself to do something you know is an authentic impulse and you have the energy to do, but you don't feel completely willing to do it. If you don't feel willing at all, don't try to convince yourself otherwise. But if you sense a little willingness, and you know you'll feel really good for having done it, coax yourself lovingly. Be encouraging and supportive of yourself, not punishing or threatening. Remind yourself why this is important to you and be willing for the experience to be satisfying.

Using authentic impulse, willingness, and energy as your criteria for deciding what to do *now* requires being very present with yourself. It requires setting aside habitual, back-and-forth thoughts such as, "I should do this, but I don't feel like doing it," so you can *sense*, directly and innocently, what is true and beneficial for you in any given moment.

The more you practice, the better you get. And the better you get, the more ease, efficiency, and effectiveness you experience in your life. Rather than jumping at the whip of your inner taskmaster, you flow with the pulse of Life moving through you. You work and rest in patterns that honor your natural, creative rhythm. You feel more rested and energized.

If your life is currently highly structured or heavily scheduled, start where you can. Identify chunks of time during which you're willing to set your to-do list aside and use these criteria for choosing what to do during that time. If you've been pushing yourself hard for a long time, taking a nap may be your only authentic impulse the first few times you experiment with this. Honor it without judgment.

And be willing to give the practice more time, so you can experience how it helps you restore balance in your life without losing *genuine* productivity. You may recognize things you've been doing that don't need to be done at all and become clear about letting them go. If you apply these criteria honestly and consistently, you may also discover the energy for creative impulses you didn't know you had. Following them will open you to greater delight and fulfillment.

This simple yet powerful practice reinforces within you the understanding that you are worthy of being trusted and treated with respect, because that's the way you're treating yourself. It also reinforces your understanding of how important your genuine preferences are, which opens you to recognizing more preferences as well as desires you may have been holding just outside your everyday awareness. I strongly encourage you to explore this practice in depth.

The open-hearted *no*

Like the previous practice, the open-hearted *no* helps you get or stay in the flow of your Life Pulse. It is an act of Self Love, one that recognizes that a *no* to what you don't want frees up the time and energy in your life for what you *do* want. And again, what you want matters.

Let me be clear that this *no* is not the same as defensively or righteously pushing against what you don't want. It isn't a "Hell, no!" It isn't about making anyone wrong. That's because it's genuinely open-hearted. While you're saying *no* to the particular opportunity, invitation or request, you're not judging it or the person who offered it. You're accepting her choice to have invited or requested you to participate, and you're choosing the response that honors the truth of what you genuinely do and do not want.

It's also a simple *no*, one that doesn't require justification. You may choose to explain that you don't have the energy or inclination to do whatever is being asked of you, or that now is not the right time, but that choice must be authentic to the relationship and not offered out of guilt.

If you're accustomed to saying *yes* to things that don't meet the criteria of being authentic to you, and for which you don't have the willingness and energy to participate, this practice may feel particularly challenging or even scary. You may have convinced yourself that saying *no* would be impolite or even hurtful to others.

Remember, we all come from the same One Source. When we honor ourselves based on our *genuine* desires and preferences, we honor the Whole. We don't benefit ourselves at the expense of others, even if they might initially see it that way. In truth, we fortify the vibration of self-honoring in the collective human consciousness, which is beneficial to everyone.

So, call on the portal of willingness, and be willing to experiment with saying an open-hearted *no* to things that you don't genuinely want to do, or have the energy or willingness to do now. Be willing to be surprised at how liberating it is, and how it can strengthen relationships through the mutual respect it conveys.

Move to neutral

One of the most challenging vibrational dynamics to understand is the impact our judgments have on our ability to realize what we genuinely desire. Most of us have strong convictions about what is right and what is wrong, not realizing that as we condemn what we believe to be wrong, we vibrate with *it* rather than with what we want.

I have committed to suspending the idea of right versus wrong. Instead, I think in terms such as wanted or unwanted, kind or unkind, and life-affirming or depleting. I hope you're willing to experiment with that as well. Even if not, I encourage you to practice suspending all judgmental, condemning, and blaming thoughts, as best you can, with the intention to maintain a feeling of neutrality.

In doing this, you are not aligning with whatever it is you dislike. You are reminding yourself that if you feel uncomfortable emotion as you focus on it, you're not in alignment with your Expanded Self or your desires. You're actually strengthening the vibrations in mass consciousness that perpetuate the very thing you wish to dissolve. Remember, we get more of what we focus on—whether it's what we want or what we don't want.

Moving to neutral, as I like to call it, is a way to describe the willingness to suspend judgmental thoughts. I've discovered that the simplicity of the phrase helps people reach a helpful stance of nonjudgment with relative ease. Often, all I need to do is tell myself to "Move to neutral, Suzanne," when I feel offended or upset by something, as I take several deep breaths. I remind myself that, in doing so, I move away from problem consciousness and toward solution consciousness.

Here are some other thoughts that may be helpful to you, as you move to neutral:

"There's a bigger picture here that I can't yet see."

"My Expanded Self has a very different perspective on this."

"Judging this won't make it go away. It will make it bigger."

"What is this showing me I strongly want?"

"The more peaceful and centered I am, the more able I am to be part of the solution."

If whatever you're observing upsets you strongly, and you feel a sense of urgency about doing something, remember that urgency almost always arises from fear. Take the time to let your uncomfortable emotions subside and settle into a neutral or, better yet, peaceful place. Then ask your Expanded Self quietly, "Is there anything here that is mine to do?" Don't rush to figure out an answer. Focus always on feeling as good as you can feel first, and trust that you will be guided with respect to what is yours to do.

This practice of moving to neutral rather than judging or blaming helps not only with judgments you may hold against others, but also judgments you may hold against yourself. If you're feeling disappointed, discouraged, or even disgusted with yourself, do your best to move it to neutral and remind yourself that your Expanded Self *does not* see you that way. Say an

191

open-hearted and very firm *no* to those thoughts and commit to finding a more loving perspective.

Remember, judgment is damaging in its assessment of something as *wrong* and therefore deserving of disdain, diminishment, or punishment. It's easy to confuse "what is" with our judgments about it. For example, it may be true that you are learning something new and making mistakes in the process, and you are far from the level of mastery you desire. But it is never true that you are bad, lazy, incompetent or any number of other withering judgments you might throw at yourself.

Move to neutral. Commit anew to loving yourself forward, with as much kindness, compassion, and support as you would offer a loved one as they venture into new territory. And commit to being as nonjudgmental of everyone else as you can. Let their words or actions remind you of what you want and keep exploring ways to bring yourself into harmony with that.

Dream interpretation

It would be difficult to overstate how immensely helpful my nighttime dreams have been to me on my journey of waking up to more and more of who I am. Because I've benefited so much from my dreams, I want to offer a brief perspective on dream interpretation.

I like to think of dreams as a nonphysical reality that co-exists with physical reality and provides information to help us see ourselves and our lives more clearly. Like our emotions during waking reality, the way we feel in dreams indicates how closely we're aligned with our Expanded Self.

The process I use to interpret a dream is, first, to describe it in writing. I do this in the morning, after I'm fully awake. I start with whatever snippet of the dream I can remember, and as I write about it, I usually begin to remember more scenes and more details. I don't analyze the dream as I'm writing, but I do *feel* for the words that best capture what I experienced and felt during the dream.

When my dream description is complete, I identify the key feelings I experienced in the dream and ask myself if I'm feeling that way in any area of my waking life. If I can easily identify the area, I then ask myself what the dream is showing me about how I've progressed, and what would be beneficial for me to see or do differently. I invite my Expanded Self to offer me the insights I'm looking for.

If the dream doesn't appear to be relevant to my waking reality, I describe it in general terms, very briefly. For example, let's say I dreamed I was driving a dear friend to her first solo performance as a pianist, but no one in my waking reality looks like her or plays the piano. I would describe the dream as, "I'm supporting a loved one in doing something that's important to her." I would go on to describe how I felt about the endeavor in the dream—perhaps nervous, or excited, or resentful, or happy for her success. At that point I usually have a ping of recognition about what the dream is revealing to me, and I once again invite my Expanded Self to offer additional insights.

I have sometimes resisted exploring the meaning of dreams that were alarming or frightening in some way, yet I've learned that those dreams often have the most supportive and encouraging of messages for me. They help me see important qualities I've developed that enable me to gracefully or powerfully navigate unexpected things that show up in life, and with that comes a sense of trust that I'm moving in the direction I want to go.

I encourage you to explore your dreams with the curiosity of an open mind and the compassion of an open heart. *Assume they are meant to benefit you* and look for their messages from that perspective. Discovering the meaning of an unusual or even confusing dream is *satisfying*. I hope you enjoy the exploration!

Meditation

The benefit of meditation on this lifelong journey of waking up to who we really are is beyond measure. When we meditate, we suspend our usual habits of thought. As our Local Self thoughts subside and we rest in the stillness of no-thought, we are refreshed by the pure, positive energy of One Source that can now flow, unimpeded, into our minds and bodies. As we gain experience with meditation, we can also use it intentionally to connect with the guidance and insight of our Expanded Self.

I strongly encourage you to experiment with various types of meditation until you find one or more that feel good to you, and that you will do regularly—ideally, every day. How frequently you meditate is of greater benefit than the number of minutes you spend meditating each time, although I encourage you to aim for fifteen minutes as you get comfortable with the experience. You can start by meditating for as little as five minutes per day.

I also encourage you to be easy with it. Don't get hung up on formal definitions of meditation and whether you're doing it "right." The essence of meditation is *intentionality*: you intend to focus your attention in a particular way for a certain amount of time. The point of focus can be your breath, an image or mantra, a candle flame, white noise, music, chants, or countless other things. If you're completely new to meditation, you may find that guided meditations set to music are a wonderful way to get started.

As with any practice, hold this lightly but with steady hands. The steadiness is in your commitment to doing it regularly. The lightness is in your approach—willing, curious, and compassionate.

Remember, the reason you do any of these practices is to lift your vibration into harmony with your Expanded Self. You do them to feel better. So, *enjoy!*

Reflection Point

Through my intentional and willing practice of new thoughts, new perspectives, and new responses to emotions, I shift my consciousness into vibrational harmony with my desires, allowing them to manifest.

12

MINDING YOUR OWN MIND

Your words are your command.

Strengthening and stabilizing patterns of thought that align with your desires generally requires practice, one of the four portals of transformation. As you think or say words, they vibrate in a way that reflects what those words mean to you. You can tell by the way you feel whether the words reflect harmony with your Expanded Self. You can, therefore, intentionally use language to evoke the feeling state you desire.

This is not the same as simply thinking or saying positive words. It is *feeling* for words that bring you into harmony with your Expanded Self. It is sincerely looking for a way to see or understand something that moves you beyond your usual habits of thought into a broader, deeper, and more loving perspective.

As a writer, I'm drawn to self-expression through words. However, you don't need to be a writer to benefit from these practices. They are not about writing beautifully, poetically, or in a grammatically correct way. Their purpose is to consciously acknowledge the power of language to shape your world and enhance your ability to use it wisely.

Reflect on concepts arising from unity consciousness

Thoughts and perspectives that are in harmony with our Expanded Self are, by definition, those that arise from unity consciousness. The unhelpful and often painful thoughts we hold, which are not in harmony with our Expanded Self or with our desires, arise from separation consciousness. If we're in separation consciousness trying to convince ourselves of something that only makes sense in unity consciousness, we won't get very far. We have to feel our way into the truth of unity consciousness.

I often think of unity consciousness as that which reflects the *deeper truth* of who we are as magnificently unique, vibrational expressions of One Source, living in a vibrational universe. In contrast, separation consciousness reflects the *surface perception* of who we are as separate physical beings, living on a physical planet with a seemingly finite number of physical resources. To develop thought patterns that bring us into harmony with our desires, we must reach for the deeper truth about ourselves and what is possible to experience. We must be willing to believe that there is a greater reality beyond that which our physical senses can detect.

In my experience, that kind of seismic shift in worldview requires focused reflection on the new perspective, with an intention to grasp, sense, know, or feel the validity of it. We have to at least be willing to believe in the new worldview before we can genuinely cultivate habits of thought that reflect it.

Years ago, when affirmations became widely known and accepted in the self-help world, people would read, write, and memorize positive statements in the hope that such statements would generate new, positive manifestations for them. Yet it's virtually impossible to believe something such as, "I have more than enough money for everything I want and need," if the worldview you've accepted is one of scarcity and limitation. Without a deeply felt understanding that this is an infinitely abundant universe, expectations of personal abundance seem impractical or even ridiculous, especially if you have repeatedly experienced not having enough of what you want and need.

Since we must *accept a thought as true* before it can become active in our vibration, we benefit ourselves enormously by cultivating a worldview in which the desired thought makes sense—the worldview of unity consciousness. The Reflection Points at the end of each chapter of this book are intended to be points of reflection to help you do this. I have consolidated them into a single list at the end of this chapter, for ease of review.

Of course, you are not limited to the Reflection Points in this book. Choose statements that inspire you, or pique your curiosity, or expand your sense of possibility—or completely blow your mind in a way that feels tremendously exciting to you. Choose points of reflection that resonate with you and ignite your desire to know more. Choose words, phrases and sentences that catalyze a powerfully felt realization within you.

I also encourage you to write reflection points in your own words, drawing on various concepts presented in this book. For example, you might create statements like these:

> My desires are innately pure and life-giving.

> As an extension *of* One Source, my desires *are* the desires of One Source.

> My purpose for being here is to allow One Source to experience itself uniquely through me, as me.

> I have nothing to prove. My worthiness is a given. I am here to express the fullness of my creativity as an extension of One Source.

Identify one or several of these kinds of statements and set aside time to reflect on them. Read them, say them out loud, meditate on them, write about them in your journal, or talk about them with someone you know and trust who also resonates with them. Imagine what your life could be like if they were true.

Here are some questions you might ask as part of your reflection:

"Am I willing to believe this?"

"Do I want to believe this?"

"If this is true, what could it mean for me and our world?"

"What evidence have I seen that this could be true?"

"How might this relate to something else I already believe to be true?"

"What makes this possible?"

I encourage you to reflect regularly on your chosen statements, perhaps weekly, and let them evolve. Consider creating groups of statements that emphasize different aspects of unity consciousness that are helpful to you for different reasons. For example, you could create a group of statements that help you stay positively focused on something new you want to create. Or you could create a group of statements to support yourself in feeling at peace where you are right now. Let your intuition and imagination guide you to the most meaningful and helpful use of your reflection points.

As you invest time in your reflection points, pay attention to how you feel. This isn't an exercise in rote reading and writing. It is an artful exploration into what your Expanded Self knows and is now coming into your Local Self awareness for you to accept with trust and confidence. Through your acceptance, you strengthen and stabilize beliefs in your Local Self consciousness that are harmonious with your desires.

Anchor statements

Anchor statements are comforting or inspiring statements of something you *already believe to be true*. Their purpose is to anchor your focus on thoughts that move you toward vibrational harmony with your Expanded Self. They can be used as reflection points, to help you further strengthen and stabilize helpful thoughts. Often, they originate *as* reflection points. The more you reflect on them, the more you feel their validity and help-fulness until you reach a point of acceptance: I believe this to be true.

Anchor statements can also be used to help you move from emotional discomfort to emotional comfort. For example, imagine that you've just been laid off from your job and you feel worried. Thoughts such as, "I'll never be able to find the kind of job I want in this economy" are swirling in your mind. Your uncomfortable feelings are a signal to pause, take some deep breaths, and acknowledge the unhelpful thoughts giving rise to those feelings.

Your intentional pause temporarily suspends the momentum of the un-helpful thoughts. But unless you focus firmly on something helpful, you may be drawn back to those same thoughts. Understanding this, you in-tentionally recall two of your favorite anchor statements and say out loud, clearly, and firmly: "I am meant to be supported in living a happy life. Something good is coming from this." As you repeat these simple state-ments to yourself, you feel a sense of calm washing over you. You have just shifted from being out of vibrational harmony with your desires to being in vibrational harmony with them.

Effective anchor statements are clear and easy to memorize and recall. They are proclamations of deeper truths that help you connect with the perspective of your Expanded Self. You can also think of them as personal mantras. They are created during thoughtful moments when you're feel-ing clear and at peace.

Because you have already accepted them as true, they have heft and mean-ing for you. When you recall them, you're reminding yourself of something helpful that you had temporarily forgotten, and you're glad for the reminder. Anchoring into something helpful makes it much easier to let go of that which is not helpful.

Anchor statements are key on the journey of shifting from separation consciousness to unity consciousness. The shift is made moment by moment and thought by thought until a tipping point is reached and your dominant thoughts become those that align with your Expanded Self on any given subject. Used consistently and lovingly, anchor statements create a stable matrix of supportive thoughts that make it easier and easier to attract more of the same.

I have created, modified, and used countless anchor statements over the years. They continue to provide stability, comfort, and inspiration to me, and they help me stay firmly yet lovingly focused on what I want. Here are examples of anchor statements that have been helpful to me and my clients and students:

I am right where I need to be.

My point of power is *now*.

I am meant to be supported in living a fulfilling life.

What I want, wants me. My desires are the desires of One Source to express itself through me, as me.

This is an infinitely abundant universe. There are countless channels through which abundance can flow to me.

I am sovereign in my world. As I think, so I create.

Vibrancy is my natural state of being as an expression of One Source. My intelligent body knows how to bring itself into balance.

There is only one true power in this universe, and it is Love. This Love is *for* me. Good is always flowing to me.

As I honor my genuine desires, I honor the Whole.

Judgment will never, *ever* get me where I want to go. Only coming into harmony with my Expanded Self can do that.

These statements only make sense within the context of unity consciousness, in which we understand ourselves to be uniquely magnificent extensions of One Source who create as One Source creates—through the power and direction of our thoughts.

I encourage you to spend quality time developing anchor statements that you intuitively know are helpful to you. To get started, simply ask yourself, "What do I *already* know or believe about myself and my creative potential that is inspiring, supportive, or comforting?" Create several of these statements, tinkering with the wording until they evoke within you a sense that, "Yes. This is true, and this feels good." And then commit them to memory.

Practice calling on one or more of your anchor statements when you notice your emotional state has dipped to an uncomfortable place. Intend to *feel* the truth of them as you think or say them. I also encourage placing one or both hands on your heart as you do so. That simple act shifts your focus subtly and powerfully to your heart, where the wisdom of your Expanded Self resides. It's also soothing and helps you release uncomfortable thoughts.

If you are a highly visual person, you might also consider creating anchor *images* that mean something important and helpful to you. For example, you might have a vivid memory of a stunning sunrise you experienced while on vacation. The memory evokes within you a deep knowing that life is beautiful and that fresh starts can occur at any moment. Calling on that sunrise image can be a loving and powerful way to anchor into the knowing, during any moment you feel stuck or sad.

201

Anchor images can be visual memories of lived experiences, artwork, photographs, or symbols that resonate with you, even particular colors and color combinations that evoke positive energy within you. As with anchor statements, effective anchor images are easy to recall and resonate strongly with you in an uplifting way. You can, of course, combine images and words to create anchors that are deeply meaningful to you.

Review your anchor statements and images regularly and be willing to modify them, set them aside, or create new ones, depending on how you're feeling about your life, and which desires you most want to realize. Use them as reflection points to help you embody their truth more fully within you. They are simple to use yet potent in their effectiveness.

Personalized prayers

If you love to read, this practice is deeply nourishing. You create one or more paragraphs that articulate the deeper truth about something important to you. I often title these written pieces, "The Truth About _____," such as, "The Truth About My Success" or "The Truth About My Health."

As with anchor statements, these longer statements only make sense within the context of unity consciousness, in which we understand that we are uniquely magnificent extensions of One Source with the power and freedom to create what we desire. I like to think of these written pieces as prayers.

Below is a prayer I wrote that has been profoundly helpful to me. I adapted it from an affirmative prayer offered by Ernest Holmes in *The Science of Mind*, combining several of his powerfully worded concepts with anchor statements and favorite phrases I had created over the years.

The truth about my success

As a unique and glorious expression of One Source, my success in every area is inevitable and assured. My Expanded Self is continuously orchestrating in-

spired ideas, opportunities, and support on all levels for my greatest satisfaction and joy, and for the realization of my desires. The Presence of my Expanded Self flows through me, inspiring me and sustaining that inspiration. I have talent and ability and I delight in using them. This talent is divinely empowered, and effortlessly attracts those who can benefit from it, in perfect timing.

Life opens to me now—rich, spacious, balanced, abundant, and beautiful. My thought, which is my key to life, opens all doors for me. I am one with Infinity, one with Divinity, and I realize this Unity. I proceed as one who knows I am abundantly guided and supported into an eternal day of divine privilege. I have only to open the portals of my soul, say yes to my desires and accept that which is ready to express through me.

Today I open these portals wide. Today I say yes to my desires. Today I am a wise and loving channel through which Life gloriously flows.

And so it is.

I love this prayer. It comforts and inspires me every time I read or say it. In writing it, I gave myself permission to claim what I genuinely wanted to experience, feeling into each sentence to make sure it truly resonated with me. I said it every day for a while, and still read or say it whenever I feel called to do so. It's like an anchor statement on steroids for me.

If this practice appeals to you, I encourage you to play with creating one or more prayers for yourself. Feel free to use this one as a starting point, or any other prayer or written piece that moves you. Tinker with it until you reach that felt sense of, "*Yes*, this nourishes my soul."

Read or say it regularly for a while, with the intention to feel its truth every time. Let it sink into every fiber of your being. Consider memorizing it, so you can call on it even when its written form isn't available to you. And most of all, keep saying *yes* to it.

Find a better-feeling perspective on something important to you

There are times when a particular aspect of your life may not be going as well as you'd like, or when something you want very much hasn't yet manifested, even though you're feeling good about your life in general. This is the practice to call on. In doing so, you acknowledge that your perspective on the situation isn't in harmony with the perspective of your Expanded Self, and you have a clear intention to shift it.

There isn't a "right" way to go about this. Your intention to feel better about whatever it is, which means your intention to move toward harmony with your Expanded Self, is where the power is. In some situations, all you need to do is acknowledge your intention, ask your Expanded Self to show you a more loving perspective, and stay open to insights and revelations that show up in meditation, journaling, or any moment in which your Local Self mind is still.

In other situations, you may benefit from consciously sorting through your thoughts to identify those that are helpful and those that are not. It's essential here to remember that only thoughts that feel good move you toward your Expanded Self. Thoughts that feel bad, even if they are "true" in the moment, keep you apart from your Expanded Self and all that you desire. So, you benefit by getting better at focusing only on the helpful ones, which means you need to identify them.

One of the most effective practices for doing this was created by Abraham and described in the book, *Ask and It Is Given*. The practice is to create a Focus Wheel, and it has helped me more times than I can count. If you don't already own the book, I highly recommend adding it to your library. It is powerfully clear and helpful. You can find a lot of information about how to create Focus Wheels online, so I won't go into how to do so here. I will say that the key to creating them effectively is to pause and feel each statement, to make sure it moves you in the direction you want to go and isn't just a nice-sounding sentence.

I spontaneously developed a technique while journaling that I've used many times, to good effect. Begin by writing down what you're currently thinking and feeling about a challenging situation, with the simple intention to record all the thoughts that have been swirling in your mind. You are neither fanning the flames of your discontent nor trying to soothe yourself at this point. You are doing your best to represent, as clearly as possible, the mix of thoughts and feelings you currently have.

The next step is to rewrite what you've written one sentence at a time, each on its own line rather than as part of a paragraph. This assumes what you wrote initially was somewhat of a stream of consciousness. (If you wrote your initial description in bullet points, you can move to the third step.)

The third step is to review each sentence individually to determine one thing: does this statement move me closer to my Expanded Self, or further away? Your answer depends on how the statement makes you feel, of course.

The fourth step is to write only the good-feeling thoughts again, either in prose or in bullet points. Reread the sentences a few times and see if you can add to them. Create a paragraph or series of statements that summarizes the perspective they reveal.

Let's look at an example of this process. Imagine that you want to experience greater financial abundance, which you've wanted for a long time. Yet each time it seems things are improving they turn in the opposite direction. You've just received an unexpected bill that you barely have the money to cover. You feel exasperated and angry and scared, all at the same time.

The next morning you sit down to do this exercise, and this is what you write:

I'm so tired of this! All my life I've struggled with money, and it's not fair. I work so hard but never seem to get ahead. I always get hopeful when I read about how people have created abundance by changing the way they think. But when I try it, it doesn't work. What am I doing wrong? Maybe it's just a bunch of nonsense, I don't think so, though, because their stories are so compelling. So, why doesn't it work for me? I just want to have enough money for everything I want and need. Is that too much to ask? It really isn't. I've got to figure this out.

Next, you rewrite the sentences or phrases one by one, in a list. Then you identify whether the statement moves you toward or away from your Expanded Self, with *Yes* representing toward and *No* representing away:

I'm so tired of this! No.

All my life I've struggled with money, and it's not fair. No.

I work so hard but never seem to get ahead. No.

I always get hopeful when I read about how people have created abundance by changing the way they think. Yes.

But when I try it, it doesn't work. No.

What am I doing wrong? No.

Maybe it's just a bunch of nonsense. No.

I don't think so, though, because their stories are so compelling. Yes.

So, why doesn't it work for me? No.

I just want to have enough money for everything I want and need. Yes.

Is that too much to ask? Not sure.

It really isn't. Yes.

I've got to figure this out. Yes.

Next, you rewrite all of the *yes* statements in one place, with a little editing if needed so they make sense as a whole:

I always get hopeful when I read about how people have created abundance by changing the way they think. Their stories are so compelling. I just want to have enough money for everything I want and need. It really isn't too much to ask. I've got to figure this out.

You read and reread this several times and reach for additional thoughts that feel good to you and that you're open to believing. Here's what you come up with:

I always get hopeful when I read about how people have created abundance by changing the way they think. Their stories are so compelling. I just want to have enough money for everything I want and need. It really isn't too much to ask. I've got to figure this out. I can figure this out, I know I can. I'll go back and find some of those stories and let myself get inspired by them. Maybe when I've tried this in the past, I didn't give it enough time. I'm willing to try again.

You've shifted from feeling discouraged and angry to feeling okay—with a little hopefulness thrown in. That's a substantive shift, and it generates enough momentum for you to become willing to experiment again with creating abundance, rather than giving up and assuming you'll always struggle.

At this point, I strongly encourage you to create several anchor statements and maybe a personalized prayer, to support yourself moving forward. There are countless types of situations in which this exercise can be helpful. The idea is to create the nucleus of a new, better-feeling perspective that you can intentionally focus on, expand, and strengthen. I have used it to feel better about people or situations that consistently frustrate me, and time and again I find that as my frustration dissipates, the situation softens and becomes a non-issue for me.

Remember, the real power in this technique lies in the power of your genuine intention to find a new perspective. The actual technique is secondary. Be willing to take responsibility for the way you feel about the people and situations in your life in a loving and supportive way. Never judge yourself for getting frustrated or annoyed or impatient. But recognize that your emotions reveal how you're *thinking* about it, and that you have the ability to shift the way you think.

You are more powerful than you know.

Ask supportive questions

Questions are a simple and useful tool for softening our limiting or painful thoughts and opening to loving ones. It's not generally easy or even feasible to jump from a painful conclusion such as, "I don't have what it takes," to a supportive one such as, "I am confident and ready to create this." An intentionally posed question can be the bridge: "What if I *do* have what it takes?"

Supportive questions are those that presume desirable outcomes and invite our minds to open to that possibility. Usually they are open-ended questions, although occasionally a yes/no question can work. They can point to a specific possibility or simply orient your focus to a generally better-feeling perspective.

Here are some examples of supportive questions:

> What if this painful thing I believe isn't actually true?
>
> What if this endeavor could be easier than I've assumed it will be?
>
> How might I see this differently?
>
> If I assume something good is coming from this, what might it be?

What if this seeming flaw of mine is actually what makes me unique?

What if this insight is valuable and I'm the perfect person to share it?

Might there be resources available to support me that I haven't recognized yet?

Is it possible that I haven't done anything wrong at all and I'm actually on the right track?

We know if a question is truly supportive by the way we feel as we ask it. I like to encourage clients to come up with several supportive questions, one after the other. Allow the first one to suggest a second, and a third. The idea is to generate momentum toward what is wanted, rather than remaining stuck on a false and limiting premise. Affirmative statements can also be included in this exercise! Here is an example:

What if I *do* have what it takes? Am I willing to believe that? Can I give myself permission to believe it? If I did, how would I feel? I'd feel excited! What if I'm the perfect person to do this? What if my passion for it is all I need to get started? There must be resources available to support me that I'll recognize along the way.

Generating supportive questions can be a fun and easy way to move your vibration into harmony with your Expanded Self. Be lighthearted about it, yet very intentional. You deserve to feel better, and supportive questions can help you get there.

Pay attention to common phrases you use

Not long ago, I was talking with a friend about a challenging international situation and how it was being addressed. It would have been easy to get carried away with judgments about all that was "wrong" with the situation, but I was committed to looking for whatever good we could see coming from it. My friend said, "Something bad always follows something good." Not wanting the momentum of our conversation to head in the direction of what frightened or angered us, I maintained my focus on what I appreciated rather than what I disliked. Happily, she joined me, referring to her presumption of something bad following something good as, "just a figure of speech."

As I reflected on our conversation later, I realized that our figures of speech are often much more than that. They usually reflect active beliefs that are taken as truths, such as, "No good deed goes unpunished," or "The bigger they are, the harder they fall." And how many times have you waited for, "the other shoe to drop?"

What makes these unhelpful thoughts easy to miss is that, because they are so familiar, they no longer generate emotions that feel uncomfortable to us. We feel emotionally "normal," which means the emotion is no longer serving its role as an indicator that we're out of alignment with our Expanded Self. The phrase feels like a throwaway, but it's likely reflecting a thought pattern in our Local Self consciousness that can generate manifested results.

I encourage you to start paying attention to the figures of speech you use, as well as any other words or phrases you say or think frequently, regardless of whether anyone else uses them. What do they reveal about your worldview and, therefore, your quality of consciousness? Be curious, not critical! This is an exercise in self-awareness.

If you identify figures of speech that reinforce concepts such as unfairness, punishment, or inescapable disappointment, become willing to suspend them. Practice pausing to take a deep breath when the impulse to say or think them arises, and then anchor into something more comforting. You might also want to create a new reflection point to counter the figure of speech with a more loving worldview and take time to contemplate it.

Hold lightly but with steady hands

Bringing your dominant thought patterns into harmony with your Expanded Self is essential to the realization of your desires. However, it's not meant to be a struggle! As with the practices I offered in the previous chapter, approach these exercises with curiosity, compassion, and creativity. At the same time, maintain a clear commitment to them. Be intentional about using them.

You are worthy of your own respect, support, and encouragement.

Reflection Point

The words I think and say vibrate with the meaning I associate with them. I can lift my vibration toward my Expanded Self by intentionally choosing language that is loving and supportive.

REFLECTION POINTS

I am a gloriously unique expression of One Source. My desires are the desires of One Source to experience itself through me, as me.

Consciousness is the primary cause of all physical effects. Physical objects and experiences exist only through consciousness and cannot be separated from it.

One Source is the only creative power in the Universe, the essence of which is unending Love. There is no other power in the Universe that can diminish or extinguish the power of One Source. I am an individual extension of One Source, imbued with its creative power.

All creative power exists in the present moment. There is no creative power in the progression of linear time. Time is the vehicle through which we perceive the unfolding of our desires.

What I want wants me. My desires already exist in the eternal Now, ready to be expressed. They become my life experience when my thoughts are in harmony with them.

As an extension of One Source, which is Love, I have nothing to fix or prove. I have the glorious opportunity to express more and more of who I really am.

I have free will. Therefore, I have the ability to cultivate beliefs that are in harmony with my desires, regardless of what others believe and experience. I am sovereign in my world.

How I feel indicates whether my thoughts are in alignment with the perspective of my Expanded Self. As I pay attention to my feelings and commit to feeling as good as I can, I come into vibrational harmony with my desires.

The clarity I need to make wise and loving choices is available through my relationship with my Expanded Self. The better I feel emotionally, the more open I am to receive its wisdom.

The energy of pure desire pulses with the power and momentum of Life itself. This Life Pulse has natural phases of expansion, contraction, and stasis. As I learn to recognize and honor each phase, my life flows with ease and grace.

Through my intentional and willing practice of new thoughts, new perspectives, and new responses to emotions, I shift my consciousness into vibrational harmony with my desires, allowing them to manifest.

The words I think and say vibrate with the meaning I associate with them. I can lift my vibration toward my Expanded Self by intentionally choosing language that is loving and supportive.

*Saying yes to my desires awakens me
to the fullness of who I am.*

AFTERWORD

Will You Stay?

About a year ago, I had a dream that was delightful and had a distinct feeling of significance. It felt more like an experience than a dream, even though none of the people in it actually exist in my waking reality. Everything was clear and vivid and felt physically real.

In the dream, I was part of a small group of friends who were preparing the space we were in for a celebration. Everyone was in a buoyant mood as we got closer to the event. I knew that a man I loved, Julian, would be coming to the party. He would only be in town for a short while before going overseas again.

Julian and I loved each other deeply. Yet he traveled extensively as part of his job and I had assumed, without ever talking to him about it, that it wasn't practical for us to make a long-term commitment to each other. I didn't want to get in the way of his success.

But as the celebration got underway, and I immersed myself in the spirit of the event, I began feeling differently. Something in me had shifted. I saw Julian across the room and our connection had never felt stronger to me. I approached him with love in my heart and found myself saying out loud, "Will you stay?"

I will never forget the look on his face when he replied immediately, "*Yes!*" It was as if he was lit from the inside. His eyes sparkled with joy and his smile was broader and happier than I'd ever seen. I suddenly knew he had been waiting for me to ask him to stay for a long time. As we joyfully embraced, our friends cheering in delight at our happiness, I felt that I had come home.

The memory of that dream came to me recently, as I was writing this book. And with it came a profound appreciation for the joy we can experience when we set aside all assumptions about why we can't have what we want and let desire itself, pulsing innocently yet powerfully in our hearts, prompt us to say *yes* to it. *Yes!*

I felt more vividly than ever the *purity* of desire and its natural, unstoppable impulse toward Life. Desire is loving, joyful, and generous. It is literally life-giving. And yet we often trample on the very thing that would transform us into the creative, magnificent, and generous people we long to be.

The paradoxical truth is that we already *are* who we long to be. Our desires are vibrational extensions of ourselves in the nonphysical, waiting patiently for us to invite them into our physical experience. We just need to say *yes* and choose to honor that *yes*. We need to *stay* with our desires, to harmonize with them, so they can manifest.

This is what I want for you. I want you to feel the power and purity of your desires. I want you to trust and honor them. I want you to embrace them with all your heart and feel excited about staying with them.

And I want you to love yourself, step by step and moment by moment, as you learn to bring your Local Self consciousness into harmony with your desires. Be steady in your commitment to doing so, but not rigid. The more lighthearted you feel, the better everything will flow.

That is one of the key messages from my dream: the happier we are, the closer we are to the thoughts and ideas of our Expanded Self. My impulse to ask Julian to stay came from the joy I felt in my heart. It was not premeditated and bore no resemblance to my usual thoughts about his traveling. It was, as our best ideas are, *inspired.*

It was inspired by desire itself, just as your desires are ready to inspire you to new thoughts and new actions that will bring them to life—to *your* life. The ideas, opportunities and synchronicities that combine to manifest your desire will unfold in perfect timing, orchestrated with mastery and delight.

What you want really does *want you*. It wants to express itself through you, as you, and it has the power and intelligence of Life itself to guide you.

You just have to say *yes*.

ACKNOWLEDGMENTS

What You Want Wants You would not exist, at this time, if not for Russell Martin.

I initially created an outline for it and drafted the first six chapters in the fall of 2019. After the sixth chapter, I felt a call to suspend many of my then-current activities, including writing, and to turn deeply inward. So, I set the book aside and declared myself to be on sabbatical. which I thought might last six months.

It lasted almost two years. And then one day, I felt the impulse to write again. I pulled out what I'd previously written and wasn't sure if I wanted to continue with it or start something completely new. Around that time, I was serendipitously reconnected with Russell Martin, someone I'd met years earlier and for whom I had great respect. I decided to work with him and sent him the outline and first chapter from my 2019 effort, explaining the two options I was considering.

On our first call, he told me in no uncertain terms that I should not abandon this book. His clarity and conviction electrified me. The haze of uncertainty I had felt vanished, and I said yes to finishing the book.

Throughout the entire process of bringing this book to life, Russell has been unwavering in his encouragement, clarity and focus. I have benefited enormously from the breadth and depth of his talent as a writer, editor and publisher, and I am honored to be published by Say Yes Quickly Books. Thank you, Russell, from my heart.

The title of this book, which I love, derives from a classic Rumi quote: ". . . what I want, also wants me . . ." Although I've often said it to clients over the years, I hadn't thought of it as a title for my book. But in an enlivening consultation with the brilliant and beautiful Kelly Notaras of KN Literary Arts, she suggested it. As soon as she did, I knew it was the title I was looking for. What I wanted found its way to me, through her. Thank you, Kelly, from my heart.

Integral to the development of this book, too, were the highly intelligent, tactful, book-loving members of my reader group: Mary Lindsey, Lynn Lyman, Lewis Maurer, Ann Murphy, Ramona Neunuebel, and Mary Schaefer. This group's earnest, loving and respectful comments helped me recognize what was valuable in my writing and what was not. I felt profoundly supported by them. Thank you, dear readers, from my heart.

One of those reader group members, Ann Murphy, has been with me from the start of my writing career. We met through our shared love of reading and writing, and she is the most literate person I know. Her love of books and film is truly infectious. She has variously been my editor, my publishing coach, my cheerleader and my friend-of-the-pen for decades. She is now a part of my family. Thank you, Ann, from my heart.

Mary Schaefer, another dear heart in my reader group, has also been integral to the development of my work. As a colleague who appreciated my writing, she recommended me for what would become a successful TEDx talk. Mary's absolute belief in the value of my work has been a deeply welcome, stabilizing presence in my life. Over time, she and I have become close friends, and our ongoing parsing of Abraham teachings is delightfully satisfying. Thank you, Mary, from my heart.

The process of turning a manuscript into a book is almost as challenging as the actual writing. Among other skills, a razor-sharp attention to detail is required, especially in the proofreading. I was blessed to have the eagle eyes, keen memory and inquisitive mind of Pam Tyson in charge of that essential task. Because of her generous heart and commitment to excellence, she actually proofread the entire manuscript twice. What a gift that was to me! Thank you, Pam, from my heart.

I had the opportunity to advance my writing skills thanks to Brian and Diane Strauss, editors of *Living.Well* magazine. Early on in the magazine's successful and highly influential life, they took a chance on me as a monthly columnist. As my writing evolved over time, they remained appreciative and supportive of it, without fail. And thanks to their magazine, my articles reached countless people I otherwise would not have reached. Thank you, Brian and Diane, from my heart.

My writing has developed, of course, through my work with the radiant souls who come to me initially as clients and students. I couldn't possibly name them all, but I appreciate each and every one of them. There are several who have been with me for a long time, and our connection has deepened my work and my writing enormously. They are kindred spirits on the path of awakening to who we really are: Joan Adelman, Sue Aigner, Megan Argo, Tris Barber, Mary Devine, Val Hollister, Vicky Kelly, Lynn Lyman, and Tracy Peal. Thank you, brilliant souls, from my heart.

My writing also reflects what I have learned and integrated from beloved teachers and authors too numerous to list. Each has added key distinctions and nuances of understanding to the immense field of spirituality and consciousness. Two of these teachers stand out as central to my personal journey and the development of what I teach: Barbara Ann Brennan, author and founder of the Barbara Brennan School of Healing, and Abraham, a collective consciousness of intelligence communicating through Esther Hicks. Their vast knowledge of energy dynamics, clarity of communication and steadfast focus on who we are as extensions of One

Source have inspired me for decades. Thank you, Barbara and Abraham and Esther, from my heart.

My beloved former coach, Tama Kieves, has been highly influential on my journey of awakening. She supported me with gentle kindness, grounded wisdom and keen insight for years, helping me create a new sense of Self after leaving the corporate world. Her perfectly timed humor could always lift me a few notches on the emotional scale, and her exquisite writing consistently brings me back to what is real and true and powerful: that which is inside of me. Thank you, Tama, from my heart.

My work, my writing and my life have also been richly blessed through my friendship with Tom Sterner. He has been in my corner for years, offering encouragement and staunch support in everything I've undertaken, particularly my writing. His mind is clear and razor-sharp, and I honestly don't know anyone as talented as he is in so many areas. I am honored to be his friend. Thank you, Tom, from my heart.

As I consider the whole of my life, and the evolution of who I am and what I create, I must express my joyful appreciation for the amazing women I am privileged to call my friends and soul sisters. Their ever-present love, respect and kindness have both buoyed and grounded me for decades. Each of them is uniquely warm, wise and wonderful, not to mention brilliantly talented. I treasure my relationship with each of them: Deborah Crane, Cynthia deLeon, Dianne Leipold, Janet Teixeira, Kathleen Quigley, and Pat Landis (who is now loving and supporting me from beyond the veil). Thank you, beautiful friends, from my heart.

Small but mighty, those of us in my family care deeply for each other. My Uncle Joe stands out as uniquely and generously supportive of my work, starting with my transition from corporate climber to energy healer, decades ago. His intelligence and generosity are rivaled only by his sense of humor, and I love him dearly. Thank you, Uncle Joe, from my heart.

My big brother, Sam, has been there for me, always. He has never doubted my talent or my ability to succeed, and he is genuinely happy for any and every good thing that comes my way. Our conversations about the awe-inspiring possibilities of space travel are always expansive and uplifting. And our shared love of a certain 2001 Dodge Stratus, named Q after one of my favorite characters in Star Trek, bonded us in a unique way that can only be experienced, not described. I am blessed that he is my one and only brother. Thank you, dear Sam, from my heart.

And, finally, I would not be who I am today without my special sister, Boo. Words such as generous, supportive and encouraging are woefully inadequate to the task of describing what a blessing she is in my life. She has never doubted the decision I made to leave a promising corporate career to pursue my dreams, a decision that seemed quite dubious at the time. She has loved me and listened to me and read—often editing and proofreading as well—virtually everything I've ever written. She has enthusiastically promoted and participated in many of my classes, and she has expertly helped me organize and run my beloved beach retreats. She is my sounding board and my spirit lifter. Our deep conversations about spirituality have significantly enriched my understanding and experience of its principles and practices. And my time with her is the time I feel most accepted, most appreciated and most loved. I feel deeply and safely at *home*. She is the best sister in the world, and she is my best friend. Thank you, dear Boo, from my heart.

ABOUT THE AUTHOR

Suzanne Eder is an an acclaimed teacher, facilitator, and mentor, as well as a leading-edge thinker in the fields of consciousness and spirituality. Formerly a successful finance director in the corporate world, she now helps people wake up to their magnificence and create lives they truly love through what she calls the Alchemy of Self-Love. She co-founded Essential Energetics, a fitness studio for women, and The SEGA Center, a holistic healing center, both of which pursuits prepared her for the in-depth client support she now offers as a teacher and mentor.

Suzanne wrote an award-winning monthly column in *Living.Well* magazine for many years, offering inspired and practical counsel in areas related to personal growth and transformation. She published the book *Ten Ways to Find Peace Rather Than Panic (When the World Has Gone a Little Crazy)* in 2009. Her first online course, "Love Yourself to Success and Fulfillment," was endorsed by *New York Times* best-selling author and self-love guru Anita Moorjani.

Suzanne has created and led many live and online classes and retreats over the past two decades, including, most recently, "Turning It All Around: Finding the Inner Truth That Changes Your Outer World;" "Riding the Waves: Navigating Intense and Rapid Change with the Grace of an Open Heart," and "The Art of Agelessness: Understanding the Power of Consciousness to Create a Healthy, Beautiful You."

Suzanne was a featured presenter at the 2015 TEDx Wilmington conference, speaking on *"The Dark Side of Self Improvement,"* a popular talk that has received more than 900,000 YouTube views, as well an acclaimed video series called *"The Alchemy of Self-Love."*

She has degrees in both accounting and economics, and she graduated summa cum laude from the University of Delaware. She began her professional career as a CPA and enjoyed a highly successful corporate career in both finance and human resources. Suzanne attended and graduated as a certified healing science practitioner from the Barbara Brennan School of Healing, an intense four-year program in mind-body-spirit health and energy healing. She also served as a mentor in the certified guide program for Divine Openings, an energy-based awakening process created by Lola Jones.

She is known among her clients, students, and colleagues as someone who easily bridges the practical and the mystical. She is deeply intuitive, wise, kind, and helpful. She lives what she teaches with integrity and humor and is, in the words of best-selling author Tama Kieves, "the real deal."

Suzanne is based in Wilmington, Delaware, USA, and is available to lead classes or workshops worldwide via video conference. She offers private mentoring in person, by phone, or video conference as well. You can learn more about Suzanne and her work at suzanneeder.com.

www.ingramcontent.com/pod-product-compliance
Lightning Source LLC
Chambersburg PA
CBHW051513120626
46551CB00012B/903